To my dear

Happy Easter!

Love,
Annabelle

The Yearbook of Love and Wisdom

To all to whom this little book may come —
Health for yourselves and those you hold most dear
Content abroad, and happiness at home.

RUDYARD KIPLING

CELIA HADDON

The Yearbook of Love and Wisdom

MICHAEL JOSEPH

LONDON

To Kitty Hobart, a good friend.

MICHAEL JOSEPH LTD

Published by the Penguin Group
27 Wrights Lane, London W8 5TZ
Viking Penguin Inc., 375 Hudson Street, New York, New York 10014, USA
Penguin Books Australia Ltd, Ringwood, Victoria, Australia
Penguin Books Canada Ltd, 10 Alcorn Avenue, Toronto, Ontario, Canada M4V 3B2
Penguin Books (NZ) Ltd, 182–190 Wairau Road, Auckland 10, New Zealand

Penguin Books Ltd, Registered Offices: Harmondsworth, Middlesex, England

First published in Great Britain 1994

3

Design and computer page make-up
Penny Mills

Printed in Singapore by Kyodo Printing

A CIP catalogue record for this book is available from the
British Library

ISBN 0 7181 3740 X
The moral right of the author has been asserted

As each day unfolds, I should like to enjoy all the good things it brings – the shafts of light into my bedroom, the delicious tastes of food, the sounds of the London pigeons cooing on the nearby roofs, or the presence of my husband as he moves about the house. These are simple but real joys I could experience every single day.

Yet too often my head is full of inner clutter – small anxieties about my daily life, recurring plans for the future, unnecessary calculations about money, obsessive thoughts about work, imaginary conversations with people with whom I feel angry, self-hurting comparisons with others.

These make me blind and deaf to simple pleasures that I could enjoy. I rush into the day. I make lists of things to do and try to do them all. I move from one activity to another trying to get things done, instead of enjoying doing them. I fight for results instead of finding pleasure in the process.

Life becomes a race, a struggle or a competition with others and I am physically, mentally and emotionally impoverished. Only by keeping the spiritual side of myself alive, can I take myself off this unnecessary treadmill.

While I wrote this book, I was trying to slow myself down so that I could live life to the full each moment, rather than rush blindly through it. I was trying to find happiness in the doing, not the results.

Some of the illustrations in this book were painted by my mother, the painter Joyce Haddon.

Celia Haddon

JANUARY

Wisdom, which is the worker of all things, taught me; for in her is an understanding spirit, holy, one only, manifold, subtle, lively, clear, undefiled, plain, not subject to hurt, loving the thing that is good, quick, which cannot be letted, ready to do good.

Kind to man, steadfast, sure, free from care, having all power, overseeing all things, and going through all understanding, pure, and most subtle, spirits.

For wisdom is more moving than any motion: she passeth and goeth through all things by reason of her pureness.

For she is the breath of the power of God and a pure influence flowing from the glory of the Almighty.

For she is more beautiful than the sun, and above all the order of stars; being compared with the light, she is found before it.

This passage from the Wisdom of Solomon places before me what I aspire to. When I fail in wisdom, as I often shall, may it be through love. For mistakes made in love are greater than wisdom.

Love is indeed heaven upon earth: since heaven above would not be heaven without it. What we love, we'll hear; what we love, we'll trust; and what we love, we'll serve, ay and suffer for too.

WILLIAM PENN

JANUARY 3

When the bald trees stretch forth their long, lank arms,
And starving birds peck nigh the reeky farms:
While houseless cattle paw the yellow field
Or coughing shiver in the pervious bield,
And nought more gladsome in the hedge is seen,
Than the dark holly's grimly glistening green –
At such a time, the ancient year goes by
To join its parents in eternity –
At such a time the merry year is born,
Like the bright berry from the naked thorn.

This poem by Hartley Coleridge speaks of hope at the new year. The cold dark winter brings a fresh start, a chance of renewal.

JANUARY 4   Fortify yourself with contentment for this is an impregnable fortress.

EPICTETUS

JANUARY

I want more and more to perceive the necessary character in things as the beautiful: — I shall thus be one of those who beautify things. I do not want to wage war with the ugly. I do not want to accuse, I do not want even to accuse the accusers. Looking aside, let that be my sole negation! And all in all, to sum up: I wish to be at any time hereafter only a yea-sayer.

FRIEDRICH NIETZSCHE

Geoffrey Stoddart Kennedy was a First World War chaplain whose poetry is forgotten nowadays. I like this verse very much.

> Peace does not mean the end of all our striving,
> Joy does not mean the drying of our tears,
> Peace is the power that comes to souls arriving
> Up to the light where God Himself appears.

Florence Nightingale, the pioneer of proper nursing, particularly loved this prayer, which comes from the end of Plato's Phaedrus.

Give me beauty in the inward soul, and may the outward and inward man be at one.

> Time is — the present moment well employ.
> Time was — is past — thou canst not it enjoy.
> Time future — is not, and may never be.
> Time present is the only time for thee.

This little verse, encouraging me to live in the day, comes from an eighteenth century watch-paper. The only time I have is now.

JANUARY 9

O man, forgive thy mortal foe,
Nor ever strike him blow for blow;
For all the souls on earth that live
To be forgiven, must forgive.
Forgive him seventy times and seven:
For all the blessed souls in heaven
Are both forgivers and forgiven.

ALFRED, LORD TENNYSON

JANUARY 10

Few people, rich or poor, make the most of what they possess. In their anxiety to increase the amount of means for future enjoyment, they are too apt to lose sight of the capability of them for present. Above all, they overlook the thousand helps to enjoyment which lie round about them, free to everybody, and obtainable by the very willingness to be pleased.

LEIGH HUNT

JANUARY 11

To me this single line at the end of a sonnet by Sir Philip Sidney is one of the most beautiful sentences in English literature.

Eternal Love, maintain thy love in me!

JANUARY 12

To cultivate kindness is a valuable part of the business of life.

This is one of the maxims of Samuel Johnson, the eighteenth-century man of letters. He practised this principle in almost all his affairs, giving time and money to all those who asked him for them.

JANUARY

One of winter's simple delights is a walk on a cold day. The poet John Clare describes the pleasures of being out of the wind.

> And O it is delicious, when the day
> In winter's loaded garment keenly blows
> And turns her back on sudden falling snows,
> To go where gravel pathways creep between
> Arches of evergreen that scarce let through
> A single feather of the driving storm;
> And in the bitterest day that ever blew
> The walk will find some places still and warm
> Where dead leaves rustle sweet and give alarm
> To little birds that flirt and start away.

Whoever is kind to the creatures of God is kind to himself.

THE PROPHET MUHAMMAD

JANUARY 15   *Darkness and depression come to us all at times. When they come to me, I try to accept them and just live through them. There is a story of Rabbi Nahum of Chernobyl (still a place of sorrows) in which he comforted his disciples with these words.*

Do not be distressed at this seeming death which has come upon you. For everything that is in the world is also in man. And just as on New Year's day life ceases on all the stars and they sink into a deep sleep, in which they are strengthened, and from which they awake with a new power of shining, so those men who truly desire to come close to God, must pass through the state of cessation of spiritual life, and 'the falling is for the sake of the rising'.

JANUARY 16   Knowledge is proud that he has learned so much;
           Wisdom is humble that he knows no more.

WILLIAM COWPER

JANUARY

He who abides in friendship abides in God.   JANUARY 17

JOHN ERIUGENA

When daisies go, shall winter time   JANUARY 18
Silver the simple grass with rime.
And when snow bright the moor expands
How shall your children clap their hands:
To make this earth our hermitage
A cheerful and a changeful page,
God's bright and intricate device
Of days and seasons doth suffice.

Lines by Robert Louis Stevenson on the seasonal beauty of winter.

For as the body is clad in the cloth, and the flesh in the skin,   JANUARY 19
and the bones in the flesh, and the heart in the whole, so are
we, souls and body, clad in the goodness of God, and enclosed.
Yea, and more homely; for all these may waste and wear away,
but the goodness of God is ever whole.

DAME JULIAN OF NORWICH

In due time, let him critically learn   JANUARY 20
How he lives; and, the more he gets to know
Of his own life's adaptabilities,
The more joy-giving will his life become.
Thus man, who hath this quality, is best.

ROBERT BROWNING

JANUARY 21

I never saw a wild thing
sorry for itself.
A small bird will drop frozen dead from a bough
without ever having felt sorry for itself.

D.H. LAWRENCE

JANUARY 22

The hill hath not yet raised its head to heaven that perseverance cannot gain the summit of in time.

CHARLES DICKENS

JANUARY 23

Edmund Waller, a poet best known for his love poems to women, also wrote a poem on divine love. Here are some lines from it.

To love is to believe, to hope, to know.
Could we forbear dispute and practise love,
We should agree as angels do above.
And love for love is all that heaven does ask:
Love that would all men just and temperate make,
Kind to themselves and others, for His sake.

JANUARY 24

This is the only profit of frost, the pleasure of winter, to conquer cold, and to feel braced and strengthened by that whose province it is to wither and destroy, making of cold, life's enemy, life's renewer. The black north wind hardens the resolution as steel is tempered in ice-water. It is a sensual joy.

Richard Jefferies' words about winter cold have a wider application. Most difficulties and disasters strengthen us.

This evening is Burns Night, a time to celebrate the birth of the great Scottish poet, who knew the importance of friendship.

The social friendly
   honest man,
Whate'er he be,
'Tis he fulfils great
   Nature's plan,
And none but he.

ROBERT BURNS

Some years back I discovered a delightful book, called The Tao of Pooh *by Benjamin Hoff. It is about the wisdom of a simple bear!*

In order to take control of our lives and accomplish something of lasting value, sooner or later we need to learn to Believe. We don't need to shift our responsibilities on to the shoulders of some deified Spiritual Superman, or sit around and wait for Fate to come knocking at the door. We simply need to believe in the power that's within us, and use it. When we do that, and stop imitating others and competing against them, things begin to work for us.

Who's this – alone with stone and sky?
It's only my old dog and I –
It's only him; it's only me:
Alone with stone and grass and tree.

What share we most – we two together?
Smells, and awareness of the weather.
What is it makes us more than dust?
My trust in him; in me his trust.

Here's anyhow one decent thing
That life to man and dog can bring;
One decent thing, remultiplied
Till earth's last dog and man have died.

SIEGFRIED SASSOON

JANUARY

A pain in the mind is the prelude to all discovery. JANUARY 28

I find this thought of Sir Almroth Wright's comforting. When I am in emotional pain, it may lead me to some valuable self-knowledge.

One today is worth two tomorrows. JANUARY 29

FRANCIS QUARLES

Cold is the winter day, misty and dark: JANUARY 30
The sunless sky with faded gleams is rent:
And patches of thin snow outlying mark
The landscape with a drear disfigurement.

The trees their mournful branches lift aloft:
The oak with knotty twigs is full of trust,
With bud-thronged bough the cherry in the croft;
The chestnut holds her gluey knops upthrust.

And God the Maker doth my heart grow bold
To praise for wintry works not understood,
Who all the worlds and ages doth behold,
Evil and good as one, and all as good.

ROBERT BRIDGES

The smallest atom of good, realized and applied to life, a single JANUARY 31 vivid experience of love, will advance us much farther, will far more surely protect our souls from evil, than the most arduous struggle against sin, than the resistance to sin by the severest ascetic methods of chaining the dark passions within us.

Wisdom from Alexander Elchaninov, a Russian orthodox priest. At times cultivating my virtues works better than fighting my vices.

FEBRUARY

Have patience with all things, but chiefly have patience with yourself. Do not lose courage in considering your own imperfections, but instantly set about remedying them; – every day begin the task anew. For, in the first place, how can you patiently bear your brother's burden, if you will not bear your own? Secondly. How can you reprove anyone with gentleness when you correct yourself with asperity? Thirdly. Whosoever is overcome with a sense of his faults, will not be able to subdue them: correction, to answer a good end, must proceed from a tranquil and thoughtful mind.

FRANCIS DE SALES

Today is Candlemas, the old church festival when candles were lit to the Virgin Mary. Some people shed light on the path for others, like candles in the darkness. The poet Henry Vaughan called them saints. This day we can remember the light-bearers in our lives.

> God's saints are shining lights; who stays
> Here long must pass
> O'er dark hills, swift streams, and steep ways
> As smooth as glass;
> But these all night
> Like candles shed
> Their beams, and light
> Us into bed.

FEBRUARY

There is as much beauty and glory in wild wetness, as in any sunlit parkland, says this poem by Gerard Manley Hopkins.

This darksome burn, horseback brown,
His rollrock highroad roaring down,
In coop and in comb the fleece of his foam
Flutes and low to the lake falls home.

Degged with dew, dappled with dew
Are the groins of the braes that the brook
    treads through,
Wiry heathpacks, flitches of fern,
And the beadbonny ash that sits over the
    burn.

What would the world be, once bereft
Of wet and of wildness? Let them be left,
O let them be left, wildness and wet;
Long live the weeds and the wilderness yet.

<u>FEBRUARY 4</u>   Every day is a messenger of God.

RUSSIAN PROVERB

FEBRUARY 5

Whether I fly with angels, fall with dust,
Thy hands made both, and I am there.
Thy power and love, my love and trust,
Make one place everywhere.

This lovely verse by George Herbert speaks to my heart. A little while ago, I started interpreting the word 'faith' as 'trust'. It has given a new meaning and hope to my spiritual life. Trust is what I need most, in order to be capable of believing I am loved by God.

FEBRUARY 6

Anyone can carry his burden, however hard, until nightfall. Anyone can do his work, however hard, for one day. Anyone can live sweetly, patiently, lovingly, purely till the sun goes down. And this is all that life really means.

ROBERT LOUIS STEVENSON

FEBRUARY 7

Lord you know we love to do things,
we are always on the go.
You know we love to make things.
Help us today to do the things that go to make up peace.

Things which cannot be measured, cut out,
pinned or stuck together.
Things like friendship, kindness
joy and love.

This prayer was written by Dudley Ractcliffe. He used it at the end of a week in which I had rushed and hurried each day, forgetting to pause for joy and friendship.

FEBRUARY 8   *The dark wet days of February are a good time to appreciate the warm rooms, cosy chairs, the comfort of familiar surroundings. Homeliness has its own joy, says the poet James Thomson:*

> Home is the resort
> Of love, of joy, of peace and plenty, where,
> Supporting and supported, polished friends
> And dear relations mingle into bliss.

FEBRUARY 9   If you endeavour to please the worst, you will never please the best. To please all is impossible.

WILLIAM BLAKE

FEBRUARY 10

> What though the heaven be lowering now,
> And look with a contracted brow?
> We shall discover, by and by,
> A repurgation of the sky;
> And when those clouds away are driven,
> There will appear a cheerful heaven.

ROBERT HERRICK

FEBRUARY 11   Also to prayer belongeth thanking. Thanking is a true inward knowing, with great reverence and lovely dread turning ourselves with all our mights unto the working that our good Lord stirreth us to, enjoying and thanking inwardly.

A passage from the medieval anchoress, Dame Julian of Norwich, an original thinker who saw the mothering qualities in God's love.

Happy times we live to see,
Whose master is Simplicity:
This is the age where blessings flow,
In joy we reap, in peace we sow;
We do good deeds without delay,
We promise and we keep our day;
We love for virtue, not for wealth,
We drink no healths, but all for health;
We sing, we dance, we pipe, we play,
Our work's continual holiday.

I can choose to follow the spirit of simplicity, described by William Rowley, in my own life. If I simplify, life gets easier.

There is a grace of kind listening, as well as a grace of kind talking.

FREDERICK WILLIAM FABER

FEBRUARY 14   *The medieval poet Geoffrey Chaucer wrote one of the earliest English Valentine's day poems. 'Make' is the old word for 'mate'.*

> Now welcome summer, with thy sonne soft,
> That hast this winter's weathers overshake,
> And driven away the longe nightes black!
>
> Saint Valentine, that art full high on loft;
> Thus singen smalle foules for thy sake –
> Now welcome summer, with thy sonne soft,
> That has this winter's weathers overshake.
>
> Well have they cause for to gladden oft,
> Sith each of them recovered hath his make;
> Full blissful may they singen when they wake;
> Now welcome summer with thy sonne soft,
> That hast this winter's weather overshake,
> And driven away the longe nightes black.

FEBRUARY 15   They know enough who know how to learn.

HENRY ADAMS

FEBRUARY

The best preacher is the human heart; the best teacher is time; the best book is the world; the best friend is God.

FEBRUARY 16

JEWISH SAYING

FEBRUARY 17

Lord, I have knelt and tried to pray tonight,
But Thy love came upon me like a sleep,
And all desire died out; upon the deep
Of Thy mere love I lay, each thought in light
Dissolving like the sunset clouds, at rest
Each tremulous wish, and my strength weakness, sweet
As a sick boy with soon o'erwearied feet
Finds, yielding him unto his mother's breast
To weep for weakness there. I could not pray,
But with closed eyes I felt Thy bosom's love
Beating toward mine, and then I would not move
Till of itself the joy should pass away;
At last my heart found voice, – 'Take me, O Lord,
And do with me according to Thy word.'

For me there is something comforting in this sonnet by Edward Dowden. There is great trust in it. Maybe evening prayer is found as much in a relaxed sleepiness as in an earnest wakefulness.

The three foundations of judgement: – bold design, constant practice and frequent mistakes.

FEBRUARY 18

This funny and inspirational saying comes from the Mabinogion, a medieval Welsh collection of tales. Mistakes worry me so much that I need always to keep this in mind – mistakes are essential for wisdom.

FEBRUARY 19 For only by unlearning Wisdom comes.

As this line by James Russell Lowell suggests, there is a kind of wisdom that comes by rejecting conventional good sense, what people will think, or the need to conform, and acting in freedom.

FEBRUARY 20

The Lord is my companion; I shall not hurry.
He helps me pause in pleasant places;
He gives me moments of renewal.
He calms my anxiety.
He keeps me in the path of quietness for His love's sake.
Yes, though I am surrounded by rush and stress and
 worry,
I will not be overwhelmed; for You are with me.
Your calmness protects and comforts me.
You have refreshed my soul even in the middle of my busy
 life.
You have eased my mind with inner peace.
Surely quietness and kindness shall follow me all the days of
 my life
And I will dwell in the care of the Lord for ever.

This modern interpretation and adaptation of Psalm 23 helps me when I am overworking and not taking care of myself.

FEBRUARY 21 In the darkest passage of human existence a Pole Star may be discerned if earnestly sought after, which will guide the wanderer into the effulgence of Light and Truth.

JOHN STUART MILL

Violets plucked, the sweetest rain
Makes not fresh nor grow again;
Trim thy locks, look cheerfully,
Fate's hidden ends eyes cannot see.

In John Fletcher's verse about violets is a whole philosophy of acceptance. We see only part, not the whole pattern of our lives.

While the Clear mind listens to a bird singing, the Stuffed-Full-of-Knowledge-and-Cleverness mind wonders what *kind* of bird is singing. The more Stuffed Up it is, the less it can hear through its own ears and see through its own eyes. Knowledge and Cleverness tend to concern themselves with the wrong sorts of things, and a mind confused by Knowledge, Cleverness and Abstract ideas tends to go chasing off after things that don't matter, instead of seeing, appreciating and making use of what is right in front of it.

More wisdom from The Tao of Pooh *by Benjamin Hoff. Living in and simply enjoying the present does not come naturally for me.*

FEBRUARY 24

When all within is peace
How nature seems to smile!
Delights that never cease
The livelong day beguile.

WILLIAM COWPER

FEBRUARY 25

If you are melancholy for the first time, you will find upon a little inquiry that others have been melancholy many times, and yet are cheerful now. If you have been melancholy many times, recollect that you have got over all those times. See fair play between cares and pastimes. Increase all your natural and healthy enjoyments. Cultivate your afternoon fireside, the society of your friends, the company of agreeable children, music, theatres, amusing books, an urbane and generous gallantry. He who thinks any innocent pastime foolish, has either to grow wiser or is past the ability to do so.

LEIGH HUNT

Lift the stone and there you will find me; cleave the wood, and I am there.

This is a remark attributed to Jesus Christ in an old papyrus — meaning God is down here with us in the world, not away up there.

Every valley drinks,
Every dell and hollow;
Where the kind rain sinks and sinks,
Green of spring will follow.

Yet a lapse of weeks —
Buds will burst their edges,
Strip their wool-coats, glue-coats, streaks,
In the woods and hedges.

Lovely verses by Christina Rossetti pointing out how the cold rain of February is what nurtures the coming beauty of spring.

No civilization is complete, which does not include the dumb and defenceless of God's creatures within the sphere of its charity and mercy.

QUEEN VICTORIA

For every ill beneath the sun
There is some remedy or none;
If there be one, resolve to find it;
If not, submit, and never mind it.

ANONYMOUS

MARCH

Yea, welcome March! and though I die ere June,
Yet for the hope of life I give thee praise,
Striving to swell the burden of the tune
That even now I hear thy brown birds raise,
Unmindful of the past or coming days:
Who sing: 'O joy! a new year is begun:
What happiness to look upon the sun!'

Ah, what begetteth all this storm of bliss
But Death himself, who crying solemnly,
E'en from the heart of sweet forgetfulness,
Bids us, 'Rejoice, lest pleasureless ye die.
Within a little time must ye go by.
Stretch forth your open hands, and while ye live
Take all the gifts that Death and Life may give.'

*William Morris] wrote these two verses. Sometimes I need to pause
and think. Is it that important? Need I rush so? What really matters? Can I find serenity in what I am doing?*

Don't be afraid to be yourself. Grow past the diminishments
and pressures of your life. Open like a flower to the love of
God. Be patient with yourself. Love yourself as much as the
Lord loves you.

*This wonderful piece of advice comes from Canon Charles Shells, who
runs Christian retreats combining prayer with art or music.*

MARCH 3   When I was driving one day with a lady on the Cotswolds, she suddenly asked, 'Do you collect barns?' For a moment I thought she meant editions of the poet, Barnes, but noticing we had just passed one of those old buildings commonly called tithe barns, I understood and replied, 'Not only barns, but churches and villages, streams and woods and mountains; in fact I am quite a landed proprietor.' For that is one way of collecting things, to lay up a picture of them in your memory ... It is the only way I collect plants; but perhaps it should be called recollecting.

This idea from the poet and botanist Andrew Young is such a good one. it brings the joy of collecting within the reach of everyone.

MARCH 4   Love is like a blossom,
Like a bee.
Love is in me.

This poem was written by Sophie Kullman when she was ten years old. If I take its last line out with me into my day, I am stronger.

MARCH

To Nature and yourself appeal,
Nor learn of others what to feel.

AUTHOR UNKNOWN

*The old calendars marked today as the first day of spring. Henry
David Thoreau celebrates the bird songs which are heard now.*

The first sparrow of spring! The year beginning with younger
hope than ever! The faint silvery warblings heard over the par-
tially bare and moist fields ... What at such a time are histories,
chronologies, traditions and all written revelations?

Why stand we here trembling around
Calling on God for help, and not ourselves, in whom
    God dwells,
Stretching a hand to save the falling man?

WILLIAM BLAKE

I am God's creature and my fellow is God's creature. My work
is in the town and his work is in the country. I rise early for
my work and he rises early for his work. Just as he does not
presume to do my work, so I do not presume to do his work.
Will you say, I do much and he does little? We have learnt;
one may do much or one may do little; it is all one, provided
he directs his heart to heaven.

THE RABBI OF JABNEH

MARCH 9

Convince a man against his will,
He's of the same opinion still;
For if he will, he will, you may depend on't;
And if he won't, he won't, and there's an end on't.

PROVERB

MARCH 10

Living my life to the full is not easy for me. The old habit of striving to get things right, rather than enjoy things as they are, takes time to die in me. I need to remember this suggestion by the Earl of Clarendon. I must not turn away from natural enjoyment.

God hath not taken all that pains in forming and framing and furnishing and adorning this world, that they who were made by Him to live in it should despise it; it will be well enough if they do not love it so immoderately to prefer it before Him who made it.

MARCH 11

From the poet Edward Young comes this warning about procrastination. I must reach for wisdom now, not tomorrow.

Be wise today; 'tis madness to defer;
Next day the fatal precedent will plead;
Thus on, till wisdom is pushed out of life.

MARCH 12

If thou desirest ease, in the first place take care of the ease of thy mind; for that will make all other suffering easy: but nothing can support a man whose mind is wounded.

THOMAS FULLER

MARCH

In every trifle something lives to please
Or to instruct us. Every weed and flower
Heirs beauty as a birthright, by degrees
Of more or less; though taste alone hath power
To see and value what the herd pass by.
This common dandelion – mark how fine
Its hue! – the shadow of the day's proud eye
Glows not more rich of gold: that nettle
   there,
Trod down by careless rustics every hour –
Search but its slighted blooms, kings cannot
   wear
Robes prankt with half the splendour of a
   flower,
Pencilled with hues of workmanship divine,
Bestowed to simple things, denied to power,
And sent to gladden hearts as mean as mine.

JOHN CLARE

Holiness does not consist in doing uncommon things, but in doing common things in an uncommon way.

EDWARD PUSEY

<u>MARCH 15</u> *Stories of the old saints show their care for all creatures. I love this tale of St Malo, translated from Latin by Helen Waddell.*

When his work was done and he came to take his cloak, he found that the small bird, whom common folk call a wren, had laid an egg in it. And knowing that God's care is not far from the birds, since not one of them falls on the ground without the Father, he let his cloak lie there, till the eggs were hatched and the wren brought out her brood. And this was the marvel, that all the time that cloak lay there, there fell no rain upon it.

<u>MARCH 16</u> They say, best men are moulded out of faults;
And, for the most, become much more the better
For being a little bad.

These lines by William Shakespeare correct my perfectionism. Shortcomings, my own and others', have to be accepted. Such acceptance may work better than vainly struggling against them.

MARCH

For St Patrick's Day, some lines said to be by the saint himself.

> I bind unto myself today
> The virtues of the starlit heaven,
> The glorious sun's life-giving ray,
> The whiteness of the moon at even,
> The flashing of the lightning free,
> The whirling wind's tempestuous shock,
> The stable earth, the deep salt sea,
> Around the old eternal rocks.

The fewer our wants, the more we resemble the gods.

SOCRATES

> All that is at all,
> Lasts ever, past recall;
> Earth changes, but thy soul and God stand sure.

ROBERT BROWNING

How happy the trees must be to hear the song of the birds again in their branches! After the silence and the leaflessness, to have the birds back once more and to feel them busy at the nest-building; how glad to give them the moss and the fibres and the crutch of the boughs to build in.

Even in towns, birdsong in the trees marks the arrival of spring. The nature writer Richard Jefferies reminds me to listen for it. In such small pleasures, so easily missed, lies happiness.

<u>MARCH 21</u>   Our greatest glory is, not in never falling, but in rising every time we fall.

OLIVER GOLDSMITH

<u>MARCH 22</u>   *The Quaker poet, John Greenleaf Whittier, wrote a long poem about the fierce blustery winds of March. Here is its last verse.*

> Blow, then, wild wind! thy roar shall end in singing,
> Thy chill in blossoming;
> Come, like Bethseda's troubling angel, bringing
> The healing of the spring.

<u>MARCH 23</u>   It has been truly said that knowledge is of the head, but wisdom is of the heart; that is, you may know a great many things, but turn them to no good account of life and intercourse, without a certain harmony of nature often possessed by those whose knowledge is little or nothing.

Leigh Hunt, the essayist, has inspiring ideas. Sometimes I need to free my mind from cleverness and knowledge. Both these smother simplicity, and get in the way of an intuitive wisdom.

<u>MARCH 24</u>

> What better fare than well-content,
> Agreeing with thy wealth?
> What better guest than trusty friend
> In sickness and in health?

Thomas Tusser wrote many verses giving advice to farmers in 1557. This verse comes from Posies for Thine Own Bedchamber.

Give not over thy mind to heaviness, and afflict not thyself in thine own counsel. The gladness of the heart is the life of a man and the joyfulness of a man prolongeth his days. Love thine own soul and comfort thy heart, and remove sorrow far from thee: for sorrow hath killed many, and there is no profit therein.

ECCLESIASTICUS

Take heed of this small child of earth;
He is great: he hath in him God most high.
Children before their fleshly birth
Are lights alive in the blue sky.

In our light bitter world of wrong
They come: God gives us them awhile.
His speech is in their stammering tongue,
And His forgiveness in their smile.

Algernon Swinburne had a special tenderness for children. Like others he saw the divine in them. We should learn from children.

Love is and was my Lord and King,
And in his presence I attend
To hear the tidings of my friend,
Which every hour his couriers bring.

Love is and was my King and Lord,
And will be, tho' as yet I keep
Within his court on earth, and sleep
Encompass'd by his faithful guard,

And hear at times a sentinel
Who moves from place to place,
And whispers to the worlds of space,
In the deep night, that all is well.

ALFRED LORD TENNYSON

MARCH 28   Each moment contains all.

JEAN PAUL CAUSSADE

MARCH 29

Thilke love, which that is
Within a mannes herte affirmed,
And stante of charity confirmed:
Suche love is goodly for to have,
Suche love maie the body save,
Such love maie the soul amend,
The highe God such love us send.

This verse is by the medieval poet John Gower.

MARCH 30

*I do not believe that unhappiness, in itself, can be good for anybody.
Yet sometimes inner change emerges after emotional pain and at a time
of unhappiness there is some comfort in remembering this, as Geoffrey
Studdert Kennedy points out.*

It is certain that we never think or strive to solve a problem
unless it hurts us to leave it unsolved, and many of us will not
move unless an unsolved problem hurts us very badly. We need
a pain, and a very sharp pain, before we are willing to face the
effort of thought.

MARCH 31

When I have faith to hold Thee by the hand,
I walk securely, and methinks I stand
More firm than Atlas; but when I forsake
The safe protection of Thine arm, I quake
Like wind-shaked reeds, and have not strength at all,
But like a vine, the prop cut down, I fall.

*What I like about these seventeeth-century lines by Francis Quarles is
the idea of trustfully putting my hand in that of God.*

APRIL

Once only in the year, yet once, does the world we see show forth its hidden powers, and in a manner manifest itself. Then the leaves come out, and the blossoms on the fruit trees and flowers; and the grass and corn spring up. There is a sudden rush and burst outwardly of that hidden life which God has lodged in the material world. Well, that shows you as by a sample, what it can do at God's command, when He gives the word.

CARDINAL JOHN NEWMAN

I love in childhood's little book
To read its lessons through,
And o'er each pictured page to look
Because they read so true;
And there my heart creates anew
Love for each trifling thing –
Who can disdain the meanest weed
That shows its face at spring?

The daisy looks up in my face
As long ago it smiled;
It knows no change, but keeps its place
And takes me for a child.

The daisies, as this poem by John Clare says, are still the same; it is we who have changed if we can no longer see their beauty.

APRIL 3

The God of love my shepherd is,
And he that doth me feed:
While he is mine, and I am his,
What can I want or need?

He leads me to the tender grass,
Where I both feed and rest;
Then to the streams that gently pass:
In both I have the best.

Surely Thy sweet and wondrous love
Shall measure all my days:
And as it never shall remove,
So neither shall my praise.

For the birthday of the poet, George Herbert, verses from his translation of Psalm 23, which tells us of a loving God.

APRIL 4 When we do not find peace within ourselves, it is vain to seek for it elsewhere.

DUC DE LA ROCHEFOUCAULD

It is a good old rule to hope for the best. Always, my dear, APRIL 5 believe things to be right, till you find them the contrary; and even then, instead of irritating yourself against them, endeavour to put up with them as well as you can, if you cannot alter them. Never anticipate evils, or, because you cannot have things exactly as you wish, make them out worse than they are.

This passage comes from a letter the essayist William Hazlitt wrote to his son, when he had taken him to his new school.

One lesson, Nature, let me learn of thee, APRIL 6
One lesson, that in every wind is blown,
One lesson of two duties served in one,
Though the loud world proclaim their enmity –
Of toil unsevered from tranquillity,
Of labour that in still advance outgrows
Far noisier schemes, accomplished in repose,
Too great for haste, too high for rivalry.
Yes; while on earth a thousand discords ring,
Man's senseless uproar mingling with his toil,
Still do Thy sleepless ministers move on,
Their glorious tasks in silence perfecting:
Still working, blaming still our vain turmoil,
Labourers that shall not fail, when man is gone.

MATTHEW ARNOLD

He who will not suffer pain, will not achieve ease. APRIL 7

GAELIC PROVERB

APRIL 8   All of the animals except man know that the principal business of life is to enjoy it.

SAMUEL BUTLER

APRIL 9   *Emily Dickinson's poems are simple, odd, but full of subtle meanings, as in this poem about spring which she wrote in 1864.*

> Spring is the Period
> Express from God.
> Among other seasons
> Himself abide,
>
> But during March and April
> None stir abroad
> Without a cordial interview
> With God.

APRIL10   It seems obvious that God, who created the world, intends the happiness and perfection of the system he created. To effect the happiness of the whole, self love in its degree is as requisite as social; for I am myself part of that whole.

William Shenstone, who wrote this passage, was an eighteenth-century poet, rarely read now. He was also a passionate gardener.

APRIL 11   What sunshine is to flowers
Smiles are to humanity.

JOSEPH ADDISON

He shall come down like showers
Upon the fruitful earth,
And love, joy, hope, like flowers,
Spring in his path to birth:
Before Him, on the mountains
Shall peace the herald go;
And righteousness in fountains
From hill to valley flow.

In the time of April showers, this verse from the hymn 'Hail to the Lord's Anointed,' by James Montgomery, has special force.

Life is not easy for any of us. What does that matter? We must persevere and have confidence in ourselves. We must believe that our gifts were given to us for some purpose, and we must attain to that purpose, whatever the price we have to pay for it.

MARIE CURIE

APRIL 14

Go thou and seek the house of prayer!
I to the woodlands shall repair,
Feed with all nature's charms mine eyes,
And hear all nature's melodies.
The primrose bank shall there dispense
Faint fragrance to the awakened sense,
The morning beams that life and joy impart
Shall with their influence warm my heart,
And the full tear that down my cheek will steal,
Shall speak the prayer of praise I feel.

ROBERT SOUTHEY

APRIL 15

There is no man who kills a sparrow, or anything smaller, without its deserving it, but God will question him about it. He who takes pity on a sparrow and spares its life, Allah will be merciful on him on the Day of Judgement.

This is one of the sayings of the Prophet Muhammad. He was tender to animals, laying down rules for their kind treatment.

Don't look for the flaws as you go through life,
And even when you find them,
It is wise and kind to be somewhat blind
And look for the virtue behind them.

APRIL 16

AUTHOR UNKNOWN

Nothing in the world can take the place of persistence. Talent will not. Education will not.

APRIL 17

This motto is in the office of one of Britain's businessmen. I think perseverance is important. I often fail to behave as well as I would like, but with persistence I shall eventually succeed, perhaps.

A cold wind stirs the blackthorn
To burgeon and to blow,
Besprinkling half-green hedges
With flakes and sprays of snow.

APRIL 18

Through coldness and through keenness,
Dear hearts, take comfort so:
Somewhere or other doubtless
These make the blackthorn blow.

A lovely poem by Christina Rossetti for the cold spell often called blackthorn winter. Hard times may stir me into a new flowering.

Enthusiastic admiration is the first principle of knowledge and its last.

APRIL 19

WILLIAM BLAKE

APRIL 20

My conscience is my crown,
Contented thoughts my rest;
My heart is happy in itself,
My bliss is in my breast.

This verse was written by Robert Southwell, a Catholic priest, in prison, where he was tortured then executed in 1595.

APRIL 21

Often we shall have to change the direction of our thinking and our wishing and our striving. That is what repentance really means – taking our bearings afresh and trying a new road. Often we shall have to allow the dynamite of life to smash up those fixed attitudes of heart and mind which lead us to make demands in their nature self-contradictory.

This comes from the writings of Harry William. Changing my fixed attitudes of mind is painful, difficult but renewing.

APRIL 22

When youthful spring around us breathes,
Thy Spirit warms her fragrant sigh,
And every flower the summer wreathes
Is born beneath that kindling eye:
Where're we turn Thy glories shine,
And all things fair and bright are Thine.

THOMAS MOORE

APRIL 23

Worry gives a small thing a big shadow.

AUTHOR UNKNOWN

APRIL

Florence Nightingale, as well as campaigning for public health, was extremely fond of cats. In a letter to a friend, she wrote:

I learn the lesson of life from a little kitten of mine, one of two. The old cat comes in and says, very cross, 'I didn't ask you in here, I like to have my Missis to myself!' And he runs at them. The bigger and handsomer kitten runs away, but the littler one stands her ground and when the old enemy comes near enough kisses his nose, and makes the peace. That is the lesson of life, to kiss one's enemy's nose, always standing one's ground.

The shortest way to God through the gate of love is found.
The road of wisdom takes you a very long way round.

ANGELUS SILESIUS

APRIL 26

I have seen the sun break through
to illuminate a small field
for a while, and gone my way
and forgotten it. But that was the pearl
of great price, the one field that had
the treasure in it. I realize now
that I must give all that I have
to possess it. Life is not hurrying

on to a receding future, nor hankering after
an imagined past. It is the turning
aside like Moses to the miracle
of the lit bush, to a brightness
that seemed as transitory as your youth
once, but is the eternity that awaits you.

R.S. THOMAS

APRIL 27   Take risks. If you win, you will be happy. If you lose, you will
be wise.

AUTHOR UNKNOWN

Think every morning when the sun peeps through
The dim, leaf-latticed windows of the grove,
How jubilant the happy birds renew
Their old melodious madrigals of love.
And when you think of this, remember too
'Tis always morning somewhere, and above
The awakening continents, from shore to shore,
Somewhere the birds are singing evermore.

HENRY WADSWORTH LONGFELLOW

Every man is a damn fool for at least five minutes every day; wisdom consists in not exceeding the limit.

ELBERT HUBBARD

I will lift up mine eyes unto the hills,
From whence cometh my help.
My help cometh from the Lord,
Which made heaven and earth.
He will not suffer thy foot to be moved;
He that keepeth thee will not slumber ...
The Lord is thy keeper:
The Lord is thy shade upon thy right hand.
The sun shall not smite thee by day,
Nor the moon by night.
The Lord shall preserve thee from all evil;
He shall preserve thy soul.

The words of Psalm 121 always sing, rather than speak, in my mind. In its music I hear the promise of a trustworthy God.

MAY

Then sing, ye birds, sing, sing a joyous song!
And let the young lambs bound
As to the tabor's sound!
We in thought will join your throng,
Ye that pipe and ye that play,
Ye that through your hearts today
Feel the gladness of the May!
What though the radiance which was once so bright
Be now for ever taken from my sight,
Though nothing can bring back the hour
Of splendour in the grass, or glory in the flower;
We will grieve not, rather find
Strength in what remains behind.

WILLIAM WORDSWORTH

The notebooks of the poet Gerard Manley Hopkins contain this passage
about bluebells. He could see the glory of tiniest things.

I do not think I have ever seen anything more beautiful than the
bluebell I have been looking at. I know the beauty of our Lord
by it. Its inscape is mixed of strength and grace, like an ash
tree. The head is strongly drawn over backwards and arched.
Then there is the straightness of the trumpets in the bells soft-
ened by the slight entasis and by the square splay of the mouth.

MAY

If spring came but once a century instead of once a year, or burst forth with the sound of an earthquake, and not silence, what wonder and expectation there would be in all hearts to behold the miraculous change.

This lovely thought comes from Henry Wadsworth Longfellow. All round me is the miracle of May. May I notice and enjoy it today.

MAY 4

If you would wish a noble life to make,
All grief o'er what's gone by forsake,
And what so may be lost to you,
Act as if you're born anew.
What each day wills, it will declare;
To your own task devote your days;
Let other's work receive your praise;
Above all else bear no man hate;
The rest to God remunerate.

THOMAS HUXLEY

MAY

Many might have attained to wisdom, had they not thought that they had already attained it.

SENECA

> The best men, doing their best,
> Know peradventure least of what they do:
> Men usefullest i' the world are simply used.

Each one of us was put in this world for a purpose, says the poet Elizabeth Barrett Browning. But many of us may never know what it was. This idea comforts me in times of apparent failure.

Our capacity to be vulnerable is not our weakness but our strength; for out of pain is born joy; and from despair, hope; and from being hated love! ... To be spiritual is to be vulnerable.

A paradox from the Catholic thinker, Matthew Fox, echoing the prayer of St Francis. I must take risks in order to love fully.

> The walks that sweetest pleasure yields
> When things appear so fresh and fair
> Are when we wander round the fields
> To breathe the morning air.
> The fields like spring seem young and gay,
> The dewy trees and painted sky
> And larks as sweetly as in May
> Still whistle as they fly.

JOHN CLARE

MAY 9 Since charity, which is benign and patient, obliges us to correct our neighbours for their failings with great gentleness; it does not appear right to alter that temper in correcting ourselves, or to recover from a fault, with feelings of bitter and intemperate displeasure.

Wisdom from St Francis de Sales. If I beat myself up with shame, I find it difficult even to admit faults. Gentleness works better.

MAY 10 Have you leant upon a gate, without a need for words,
To take in Nature's wonder, and to listen to the birds?
Yes, leaning on a gate is a thing we ought to do.
It helps us to unwind and such moments are so few.
An anonymous commonplace verse to remind me to slow down.

MAY 11 *The Prophet Muhammad was once asked which deeds are most loved by God. His reply, paraphrased here, was very shrewd.*

The deeds most loved by God are the regular and habitual ones, even if they are few. Don't take things upon yourself, unless they are things which are within your abilities to carry out.

MAY 12 Each star, to rise, and sink, and fade –
Each bird that sings its song and sleeps –
Each spark of spirit fire that leaps
Within me – of One Flame are made!

JOHN GALSWORTHY

My favourite new hymn was written by Gerard Markland from a passage in Isaiah, and speaks of God's care for each individual.

Do not be afraid,
for I have redeemed you.
I have called you by your
    name;
you are mine.

When you walk through the
    waters, I'll be with you.
you will never sink beneath
    the waves.

When the fire is burning all
    round you,
you will never be consumed by the
    flames.

When the fear of loneliness is looming,
then remember I am at your side.

You are mine, O my child; I am your Father,
and I love you with a perfect love.

If a thing's worth doing, it's worth doing badly.

G.K. CHESTERTON

MAY 15   For it needeth us to fall, and it needeth us to see it. For if we never fell, we should not know how feeble and how wretched we are of our self, and also we should not fully know that marvellous love of our Maker. For we shall see verily in heaven, without end, that we have grievously sinned in this life, and notwithstanding this, we shall see that we were never hurt in His love, we were never the less of price in His sight.

DAME JULIAN OF NORWICH

MAY 16   *I love this prayer in poetry by Henry Vaughan.*
Deceptively simple, it asks for what I need most.
If only I could start each day with a quiet mind and the
plain heart of a happy child within me!

Give me humility and peace,
Contented thoughts, innocuous ease,
A sweet, revengeless, quiet mind,
And to my greatest haters, kind.
Give me, my God! a heart as mild
And plain as when I was a child.

MAY

Peace I leave with you; my peace I give unto you. Not as the world giveth, give I unto you. Let not your heart be troubled neither let it be afraid.

JESUS OF NAZARETH

One of my frequent failings is to rush to give solutions to people who just need sympathy. The Revd Charles Colton puts it this way:

It is always safe to learn, even from our enemies; seldom safe to instruct even our friends.

> He who gives a child a treat
> Makes joy-bells ring in Heaven's street,
> And he who gives a child a home
> Builds palaces in Kingdom Come,
> And she who gives a baby birth
> Brings Saviour Christ again to earth;
> For life is joy, and mind is fruit,
> And body's precious earth and root.

JOHN MASEFIELD

Can you tell me how to build a happy home? Integrity must be the Architect, Tidiness the Upholsterer. It must be warmed by Affection, lighted up with Cheerfulness. Industry must be the Ventilator. But the greatest requisite of all is The Sunshine from Above.

These quaint words come from a Victorian valentine. I wonder if tidiness matters (for I am very untidy) but the rest rings true.

MAY 21   *Common hedgerow bushes and roadside plants have their own beauty. Algernon Swinburne wrote this about the hawthorn.*

> The coming of the hawthorn brings on earth
> Heaven; all the spring speaks out in one sweet word,
> And heaven grows gladder, knowing earth has heard.
> Ere half the flowers are jubilant in birth,
> The splendour of the laughter of their mirth
> Dazzles delight with wonder.

MAY 22   A friend is a present you give yourself.

ROBERT LOUIS STEVENSON

MAY 23

> I have received a Power infinitely greater
> Than that both of creating and enjoying worlds;
> Infinitely more blessed, profitable, divine, glorious.
> O Lord, I am contented with my being.
> I rejoice in Thine infinite bounty,
> And praise Thy goodness.
> I see plainly that Thy love is infinite.

THOMAS TRAHERNE

MAY 24   It is said of the large-hearted John Wesley, that on one occasion, when a fly pitched on the back of his hand, instead of crushing the life out of it (which is too often done by some people) he gently brushed it off, saying as he did so: 'Go, sir; there is room enough for both of us.'

VERNON MORWOOD

Hark to the thrush ...   <u>MAY 25</u>
How eloquently well he tells his tale
That love is yet on earth, and yet will be,
Though virtue struggles and seems born to fail.
Then for thy sake, I will not loathe man's face;
Will not believe that virtues are veiled sins;
That beauty may be mean and kindness base;
That fortune plays the game which wisdom wins;
That human worth still ends where it begins.
Though man were wholly false, though hope were none
Of late redemption from his sin-made woes,
Yet would I trust in God and goodness. On
From sun to sun the stream of mercy flows
And still on humble graves the little daisy grows.

EBENEZER ELLIOTT

We must have our times for companionship with God.   <u>MAY 26</u>

WILLIAM TEMPLE

There's nothing in the world, I know,
That can escape from love,
For every depth it goes below,
And every height above.

It waits, as waits the sky,
Until the clouds go by,
Yet shines serenely on
With an eternal day,
Alike when they are gone,
And when they stay.

Implacable is love,
Foes may be bought or teased
From their hostile intent,
But he goes unappeased
Who is on kindness bent.

HENRY DAVID THOREAU

MAY

It's never too late to have a happy childhood.

AUTHOR UNKNOWN

When a bird flips his tail in getting his balance on a tree
He feels much gayer than if somebody had left him a fortune
Or than if he'd just built himself a nest with a bathroom —
Why can't people be gay like that?

MAY 29

D. H. LAWRENCE

We have first to learn to love ourselves, because, without such
generous love of self, our love for others becomes, whatever its
outward manifestations, in its inner essence a compulsive grasp-
ing in which we try to compensate from their personality for the
value which we deny to our own.

MAY 30

HARRY WILLIAMS

My mind lets go a thousand things
Like dates of wars and deaths of kings,
And yet recalls the very hour —
'Twas noon by yonder village tower,
And on the last blue noon in May —
The wind came briskly up this way,
Crisping the brook beside the road;
Then, pausing here, set down its load
Of pine-scents, and shook listlessly
Two petals from that wild rose tree.

MAY 31

THOMAS BAILEY ALDRICH

JUNE

Now summer is in flower, and nature's hum
Is never silent round her bounteous bloom;
Insects, as small as dust, have never done
With glittering dance, and reeling in the sun;
And green wood fly, and blossom-haunting bee,
Are never weary of their melody.
Round field and hedge, flowers in full glory twine,
Large bindweed bells, wild hop, and streaked woodbine,
That lift athirst their slender-throated flowers,
Agape for dew falls, and for honey showers;
These o'er each bush in sweet disorder run,
And spread their wild hues to the sultry sun.

*John Clare's poem about June reminds me of the enjoyments of this
month. Even in parks and suburbs there are summer bees and insects,
and where the grass is unmown, summer flowers.*

He brought light out of darkness, not out of a lesser light; he
can bring thy summer out of winter though thou have no
spring; though in the ways of fortune, or understanding, or conscience, thou have been benighted till now, wintered and frozen,
clouded and eclipsed, smothered and stupefied till now, now
God comes to thee, not as in the dawning of the day, not as in
the bud of spring, but as the sun at noon.

JOHN DONNE

JUNE 3

The lilies of the field whose bloom is brief;
We are as they;
Like them we fade away
As doth a leaf.

Consider
The sparrows of the air of small account;
Our God doth view
Whether they fall or mount, —
He guards us too.

CHRISTINA ROSSETTI

JUNE 4 If you become really interested in other people you will make more friends in two months than you would in two years by trying to get other people interested in you.

I do not know who said this but I wrote it down on a piece of paper at the time. To be effective, making friends needs a genuine interest in others. When I fake concern, I am usually found out.

JUNE

True wisdom is to be always seasonable, and to change with a good grace in changing circumstances. To love playthings well as a child, to lead an adventurous and honourable youth, and to settle when the time arrives, into a green and smiling age, is to be a good artist in life and deserve well of yourself and your neighbour.

I need this piece of advice from Robert Louis Stevenson, for I find it difficult to change in a changing world. I fear all change and thus I find it hard to accept change and to remain flexible to it.

Be useful where thou livest, that they may
Both want and wish thy pleasing presence still.
Kindness, good parts, great places are the way
To compass this. Find out men's wants and will,
And meet them there. All worldly joys go less
To the one joy of doing kindnesses.

GEORGE HERBERT

Let your mind drift over the day, refraining from any self-judgement, whether of approval or disapproval, attending to and relishing only those moments of the day for which your are grateful. Even the most harrowing day includes some good moments, if only we take the trouble to look – it might be the sight of a raindrop falling, or the fact that I can see at all ... This daily review of consciousness is an exercise in the 'praise, reverence and service of God'.

GERALD W. HUGHES

JUNE 8

Blest power of sunshine! genial day,
What balm, what life is in thy ray!
To feel thee is such real bliss
That had the world not joy but this,
To sit in sunshine calm and sweet,
It was a world too exquisite
For man to leave without regret.

This verse by Thomas Moore, a poet of the eighteenth century, reminds me of a simple pleasure — another joy to enrich my life.

JUNE 9   If I am not myself, who else will be?

This short sentence by the American writer, Henry David Thoreau, means a lot to me. Too often, I compare myself with others to my disadvantage. I need to accept myself as I am.

JUNE 10

Vain is the glory of the sky,
The beauty vain of field and grove,
Unless, while with admiring eye
We gaze, we also learn to love.

WILLIAM WORDSWORTH

JUNE 11   Heavy thoughts bring on physical maladies; when the soul is oppressed, so is the body. But when the heart is at rest, and quiet, then it takes care of the body. Therefore we ought to abandon and resist anxious thoughts by all possible means.

MARTIN LUTHER

The rose is without why.
It blows because it blows.
It thinks not of itself
And no display it shows.

ANGELUS SILESIUS

A butterfly comes and stays on a leaf – a leaf much warmed by the sun – and shuts his wings. In a minute he opens them, shuts them again, half wheels round, and by and by – just when he chooses and not before – floats away. The flowers open, and remain open for hours, to the sun. Hastelessness is the only word one can make up to describe it; there is much rest, but no haste. Each moment is so full of life that it seems so long and so sufficient in itself. Not only the days, but life itself lengthens in summer. I would spread abroad my arms and gather more of it to me, could I do so.

The writer Richard Jefferies describes a kind of mysticism he found in nature. Even in a busy working day, I can pause and reconnect to the spiritual, rather than temporal, life around me.

JUNE 14

Teach both mine eyes and feet to move
Within those bounds set by Thy love;
Grant I may soft and lowly be,
And mind those things I cannot see ...
Let me Thy ass be, only wise
To carry, not search mysteries;
Who carries Thee is by Thee led
Who argues, follows his own head ...
And when (O God!) the ass is free
In a state known to none but Thee;
O let him by his Lord be led,
To living springs, and there be fed
Where light, joy, health and perfect peace
Shut out all pain and each disease.

Let us be like the humble donkey, says the poem by Henry Vaughan. I love these modest beasts, who have played their part in great religious mysteries. For me they are a moving example.

JUNE 15 Every man in his lifetime needs to thank his faults.

RALPH WALDO EMERSON

JUNE 16

Did ever any trust in the Lord, and was confounded?
Or did any abide in his fear, and was forsaken?
Or whom did He ever despise that called upon him?
For the Lord is full of compassion and mercy, long suffering and very pitiful and forgiveth sins.

ECCLESIASTICUS

JUNE 17

Benjamin Franklin kept a special note of his daily faults, and worked on a different virtue each week. He used this prayer daily.

O powerful Goodness! bountiful Father! merciful Guide! Increase in me that wisdom which discovers my truest interest. Strengthen my resolutions to perform what that wisdom dictates. Accept my kind offices to Thy other children as the only return in my power for Thy continual favours to me.

JUNE 18

If solid happiness we prize,
Within our breast this jewel lies,
And they are fools who roam:
The world has nothing to bestow,
From our own selves our joys must flow,
And that dear hut, our home.

Charles Cotton wrote a poem called 'The Fireside', containing these lines. They are a reminder of the comforting pleasures of a home.

JUNE 19

The truth is that everything is a miracle and wonder.

RABBI BARUKH

JUNE 20

Give to the world the best that you have,
And the best will come back to you,
Give of the friendship that all men crave
And your friends will be many and true.
Give love, and love to your life will flow
A strength in your utmost need,
Give faith, and a score of friends will show
Their faith in your word and deed.

This anonymous verse came on a Christmas card from a friend of mine, William Donald, a man of courage, humour and endurance.

JUNE 21

The seat of knowledge is in the head; of wisdom, in the heart. We are sure to judge wrong if we do not feel right.

WILLIAM HAZLITT

JUNE 22

Enable with perpetual light
The dullness of our blinded sight.

These two lines from Bishop Cosin's hymn strike a chord with me. When light enters in on my own darkness, I am given new power.

JUNE 23

Love is the true means by which the world is enjoyed. Our love to others, and others' love to us. We ought therefore above all things to get acquainted with the nature of love. For love is the root and foundation of nature; love is the soul of life and crown of rewards.

THOMAS TRAHERNE

Sweet babe, in thy face
Holy image I can trace.
Sweet babe, once like thee,
Thy maker lay and wept for me.

Wept for me, for thee, for all,
When he was an infant small
Thou his image ever see,
Heavenly face that smiles on thee.

Smiles on thee, on me, on all;
Who became an infant small.
Infant smiles are his own smiles;
Heaven and earth to peace beguiles.

WILLIAM BLAKE

JUNE 24

To repress our wonder is to kill our capacity for the divine.   JUNE 25

This was written by Matthew Fox, a Catholic priest who writes about a spirituality centred on this life, rather than the next.

JUNE 26   *St Francis, the saint who treated all creation as his family, cared for every being. Thomas of Celano describes his love of bees and flowers.*

Their nimble activity and their wondrous science could move him to glorifying the wonders of the Lord so enthusiastically that he often would speak of nothing else for a whole day, praising the bees and the other creatures ... When he found many flowers growing together, it might happen that he would speak to them and encourage them, as though they could understand, to praise the Lord.

JUNE 27   It is easier to be angry than to pity,
it is easier to condemn than to understand,
easier to find the Uncelestial City
than the dim counties of the Holy Land.

HUMBERT WOLFE

He that judges not well of the importance of his affairs, though he may be always busy, he must make but small progress. But make not more business necessary than is so; and rather lessen than augment work for thyself.

The Quaker writer, William Penn, admitted the temptation to make work. To be able to distinguish between the important and the merely urgent, and make time for the former, is a great gift.

Man is not God but hath God's end to serve,
A master to obey, a course to take,
Somewhat to cast off, somewhat to become?
Grant this, then man must pass from old to new,
From vain to real, from mistake to fact,
From what once seemed good, to what now proves best.
How could man have progression otherwise?

ROBERT BROWNING

Since the stars of heaven do differ in glory; since there are some stars so bright that they can hardly be looked on, some so dim that they can scarce be seen, and vast numbers not to be seen at all by artificial eyes; read thou the earth in heaven, and things below from above. Look contentedly upon the scattered difference of things, and expect not equality in lustre, dignity, or perfection in regions or persons below.

Sir Thomas Browne recognized the pain we give ourselves by comparing our selves or our circumstances with those of others.

JULY

And God is the weight that bends the bough
Of the young tree gently as spring snow.
His is the lightness on the summer flower
Of the bee's touch, and his the power
That tames the sea and poises like a feather
Or a loose leaf the world. He threads together
The stars for necklace and his glory shows,
Then hides himself within the cloistered rose.

The poems of R.S. Thomas, a Welsh poet, are a delight to me. This month in gardens or city parks and gardens I can see God in a rose.

When Queen Victoria's favourite spaniel died, she buried him with a touching epitaph. He had been her loving companion from childhood, and had been with her when she ascended the throne. Animals often seem to have, by way of their natures and without effort, spiritual gifts for which we humans have to struggle.

Here lies Dash, the Favourite Spaniel of her Majesty Queen Victoria, by whose command this Memorial was Erected. He died on the 20th December, 1840, in his 9th year.

> His attachment was without selfishness,
> His playfulness without malice,
> His fidelity without deceit.

Reader, if you would live beloved and die regretted, profit by the example of Dash.

JULY 3

'Nature' is what we see –
The Hill – the Afternoon –
Squirrel – Eclipse – the Bumble bee –
Nay – Nature is Heaven–
Nature is what we hear –
The Bobolink – the Sea
Thunder – the Cricket –
Nay – Nature is Harmony –
Nature is what we know –
Yet have no art to say –
So impotent Our Wisdom is
To her Simplicity.

A wonderful nature poem by Emily Dickinson. The bobolink is an American bird with bright plumage and a bubbling spring song.

JULY 4   None of you will have real faith until you wish for your brother what you want for yourself.

THE PROPHET MUHAMMAD

Contempt is a defensive reaction.

Since I heard this, I have understood that when I despise another human being, that feeling says as much about me, as about them. There is fear in the feeling. It often means that I feel threatened.

> Each day the world is born anew
> For him who takes it rightly.

JAMES RUSSELL LOWELL

He who rightly understands himself will never mistake another man's work for his own, but will attend to himself, and above all improve the faculties of his mind, will refuse to engage in useless employments, and will get rid of all unprofitable thoughts and schemes.

This piece of wisdom from the essayist Michel Montaigne reminds me to focus on myself. Alas, I often feel I have solutions for others, forgetting to leave them the dignity of finding their own answers.

> It is the mind that maketh good or ill,
> That maketh wretch or happy, rich or poor:
> For some, that hath abundance at his will,
> Hath not enough, but wants in greatest store,
> And other, that hath little, asks no more,
> But in that little is both rich and wise;
> For wisdom is most riches.

EDMUND SPENSER

JULY 9

Teach me delight in simple things
And mirth that has no bitter springs;
Forgiveness free of evil done,
And love to all men 'neath the sun.

RUDYARD KIPLING

JULY 10

Lighten my darkness, Lord. When your light comes first into my life, it makes the shadows in my heart look darker and I am dismayed. In the darkness, I could not see how black my life was. As the light continues, I can slowly learn to banish some of those shadows by taking clarity into the dark corners of my heart. So lighten my darkness, Lord.

AUTHOR UNKNOWN

JULY 11

To thine own self be true;
And it must follow, as the night the day,
Thou canst not then be false to any man.

These lines by William Shakespeare remind me that real honesty, in all I say, as well as do, protects me and others. My nature is so fearful that I often lie to please others or to avoid their anger.

JULY 12

Rest is not idleness, and to lie on the grass under the trees on a summer's day, listening to the murmur of water, or watching the clouds float across the sky, is by no means a waste of time.

JOHN LUBBOCK

JULY

Do the work that's nearest,
Though it's dull at whiles,
Helping, when we meet them,
Lame dogs over stiles.

*In youth I used to sneer at these
rather clichéd lines by Charles
Kingsley; now I'm older, I think
they sum up a good way to live.*

*Five hundred years ago schoolboys were given English sentences to
translate into Latin. In a Tudor textbook from Oxford comes this
charming passage about the joys of early rising in summer.*

It is a world to see the delectation and pleasure that a man shall
have which riseth early in these summer mornings, for the very
dew shall be so comfortable to him that it shall cause him
inwardly to rejoice. Beside that, to hear the birds sing on every
side, the lark, the jays, the sparrow, with many other, a man
would think he had a heavenly life. Who would then lie thus
loitering in his bed, brother, as thou dost, and give himself only
to sleep, by the which thou shalt hurt greatly thyself and also
shorten the time of thy life?

<u>JULY 15</u>

Nobody made a greater mistake than he who did nothing because he could only do a little.

Wisdom from Edmund Burke. It's natural to feel that because we cannot do much, nothing is worth doing. But every little counts.

<u>JULY 16</u>

Now the glories of the year
May be viewed at the best,
And the earth doth now appear
In her fairest garments drest.
Sweetly smelling plants and flower
Do perfume the garden bowers;
Hill and valley, wood and field,
Mixed with pleasures, profits yield.

Other blessings, many more
At this time enjoyed be;
And in this my song, therefore,
Praise I give, O Lord, to thee.

GEORGE WITHER

JULY

Clear Thou my paths, or shorten Thou my miles,
Remove the bars, or lift me o'er the stiles;
Since rough the way is, help me when I call,
And take me up, or else prevent the fall.

These are lines from a poem by Robert Herrick.

Childhood often holds a truth with its feeble fingers, which the grasp of manhood cannot retain, which it is the pride of utmost age to recover.

JOHN RUSKIN

May I through life's uncertain tide
Be still from pain exempt;
May all my wants be still supplied;
My state too low to admit of pride,
And yet above contempt.

But should Thy providence divine
A greater bliss intend,
May all these blessings you design,
If e'er those blessings shall be mine,
Be centred in a friend.

JAMES MERRICK

The commonest objects are only wonders at which habit has made us cease to wonder.

LEIGH HUNT

JULY 21

> Anger in its time and place
> May assume a kind of grace.
> It must have some reason in it,
> And not last beyond a minute.

Charles and Mary Lamb wrote these lines for children and for people like me. I often deny my anger to myself and it goes underground and simmers. Acknowledging my anger tames it.

JULY 22   The sense of sight is indeed the highest bodily privilege, the purest physical pleasure which man has derived from his Creator.

Some people, including perhaps Sydney Smith, the author of these words, have a natural joy in sight. I have to remember and cultivate mine, otherwise I live blindly, missing the beauty.

JULY 23

> What matters though I doubt at every pore,
> Head-doubts, doubts at my fingers' ends,
> Doubt in the trivial work of every day,
> Doubts at the very bases of my soul ...
> It is the idea, the feeling and the love,
> God means mankind should strive for and show forth.

ROBERT BROWNING

JULY 24   Gratitude is heaven itself; there could be no heaven without gratitude; I feel it and I know it. I thank God and man for it.

WILLIAM BLAKE

Today is
the Tomorrow
you worried
about
Yesterday.

MOTTO ON A SUNDIAL

The sovereign voluntary path to cheerfulness, if our spontaneously cheerfulness be lost, is to sit up cheerfully, to look round cheerfully, and to act and speak as if cheerfulness were already there. If such conduct does not make you soon feel cheerful, nothing else on that occasion can. So to feel brave, act as if we were brave, use all our will to that end, and a courage-fit will very likely replace the fit of fear.

This is the 'As if' principle, put forward by William James. There are times when it does not apply, when we need to feel feelings. But for facing the rough and tumble of ordinary life, it can be a help. When I tell myself I am brave, it is easier to be so.

<u>JULY 27</u>

O dreamy, gloomy, friendly trees,
I came along your narrow track
To bring my gifts unto your knees
And gifts you did bring back;
For when I brought this heart that burns –
These thoughts that bitterly repine –
And laid them here among the ferns,
And the hum of boughs divine,
Ye vastest breathers of the air,
Shook down with slow and mighty poise
Your coolness on the human care,
Your wonder on its toys,
Your greenness on the heart's despair,
Your darkness on its noise.

HERBERT TRENCH

<u>JULY 28</u>   Things which are impossible with men are possible with God.

JESUS OF NAZARETH

It is a serious disease to worry about what has not occurred.

IBN GABIROL

> Where does the wisdom and the power divine
> In a more bright and sweet reflection shine?
> If we could open and intend our eye,
> We all, like Moses, should espy
> Ev'n in a bush the radiant Deity.

Another poet, this time Abraham Cowley in a poem about gardens, points out that we can see God as easily down here as up there.

A touching story about saints and animals concerns St Anthony of   *Padua, when he preached near a river bank. Such stories tell us of the fellowship, not just of human, but of all living beings.*

And there came to the bank where he stood a multitude of fishes, great, small and middling, more than had ever been seen on that coast or in that river. And they all stretched their heads out of the water and turned attentively towards the face of St Anthony, all in great peace, gentleness and orderliness. For the smallest fishes were in front, by the bank, and behind them the middling ones, and at the back where the water was deeper, the biggest fishes. When the fishes were thus placed in order and array, St Anthony began to preach solemnly and said, 'O Fishes, my brothers, you are bound, according to your means to render great thanks to our Creator.'

AUGUST

As I was walking there, and looking up on the sky and clouds, there came into my mind so sweet a sense of the glorious majesty and grace of God that I know not how to express. My sense of divine things gradually increased, and became more and more lively, and had more of that inward sweetness. The appearance of everything was altered; there seemed to be, as it were, a calm, sweet cast, or appearance of divine glory in almost every thing. God's excellency, his wisdom, his purity and love, seemed to appear in every thing; in the sun, moon, and stars; in the clouds and blue sky; in the grass, flowers, trees; in the water and all nature.

This passage was written by Jonathan Edwards, the eighteenth-century American theologian. This month, when we have time to relax from work, is a good time to notice God's glory around us.

How various his enjoyments, whom the world
Calls idle; and who justly in return
Esteems that busy world an idler too!
Friends, books, a garden, and perhaps his pen,
And nature in her cultivated trim
Dressed to his taste, inviting him abroad
Can he want occupation who has these?
Will he be idle, who has much t'enjoy?

WILLIAM COWPER

<u>AUGUST 3</u>

In the morning early
I go down to the sea
And see the mist on the shore;
I listen, and I listen.
When I go to the rocks
I go looking for shells
And feel the sand beneath my feet;
I listen, and I listen.
I sometimes think that God
Is talking to me
When I hear the sound of the sea;
I listen, and I listen.
I listen and I listen.

These lines come from a children's hymn by Hazel Charlton. Pausing and listening hard whether by the sea, in the country or even in the town, quietens my mind. In listening there is a kind of serenity.

<u>AUGUST 4</u>   Trust thyself; every heart vibrates to that iron string.

RALPH WALDO EMERSON

AUGUST

Keeping the mind too long upon one thing is like standing too long in one posture.

This reminder comes from the Marquis of Halifax. When I worry about something, my thinking almost always becomes distorted.

O run for wisdom not,
Nor wit, across the sea.
On love alone depends
The soul's true dignity.

ANGELUS SILESIUS

Failure is instructive. The person who really thinks, learns quite as much from his failures as from his successes.

JOHN DEWEY

With all, as in some rare limned book, we see
Here painted lectures of God's sacred will.
The daisy teacheth lowliness of mind,
The camomile, we should be patient still;
The rue our hate of vice's poison ill;
The woodbine, that we should our friendship hold;
Our hope the savory in the bitterest cold.

This is an old-fashioned idea, that herbs can teach us virtue, from an Elizabethan poet, Henry Peacham. Yet why not? Perhaps if I thought of their virtues when I see the herbs and daisies in my garden, it might remind me to cultivate these virtues in myself.

AUGUST 9

Come, be happy! lie thee down,
On the fresh grass newly mown,
Where the grasshopper doth sing
Merrily – one joyous thing
In a world of sorrowing.

Poets like Percy Bysshe Shelley remind us of commonplace joys. There is new mown grass smelling heavenly even in a city park.

AUGUST 10

Children are not put here for us to teach. They are put on this world for us to learn from. We don't teach them; they teach us.

BOB EARLL

AUGUST 11

The great command will never be obsolete:
Know Thyself.
New life bubbles in, we become something else,
Something we have not been, and therefore cannot
      yet know.

D.H. LAWRENCE

AUGUST 12

Stoop and touch the earth, and receive its influence; touch the flower, and feel its life; face the wind, and have its meaning; let the sunlight fall on the open hand as if you could hold it. Something may be grasped from them all, invisible yet strong. It is sense of a wider existence – wider and higher.

RICHARD JEFFERIES

AUGUST

From Trevor Stephens of the Lani Memorial Trust, which helps village development in India, comes this Hindu story about trying.

A little sparrow tries to drink the ocean dry with her beak, because the ocean has taken her eggs and refuses to return them. Other birds look on in amazement at such an impossible task which the little sparrow has set herself. Finally Garuda, the giant eagle devotee who carries Lord Vishnu on his back, arrives on the scene feeling great compassion towards his little sister-bird. With the divine authority of Lord Vishnu Himself, Garuda commands the ocean to return the eggs and, in fear and trembling, the ocean obliges immediately. But it would not have happened if the little sparrow had not tried to do the impossible.

Thou must not be over sorrowful;
Better to trust in God than to forebode ill.

TALIESIN, THE WELSH BARD

AUGUST 15 Animals bring humour into our lives, a radical, celebrative awareness of dialectic and paradox. Animals, I am convinced, love to make us human animals laugh. They are often well aware, in my opinion, of what makes us laugh and they are very often as humorous as they are humour-bearers. Animals are truly holy in their way, for all full humour is reflection of the divine good humour.

MATTHEW FOX

AUGUST 16

What Thou shalt today provide,
Let me as a child receive;
What tomorrow may betide,
Calmly to Thy wisdom leave;
'Tis enough that Thou wilt care:
Why should I the burden bear?

I try, and often fail, to live in the day not worrying about the future, as this verse from a hymn by John Newton recommends.

AUGUST

In every speck of dust are Buddhas without number. AUGUST 17

AUTHOR UNKNOWN

    How gently, beautiful and calm,   AUGUST 18
    The quiet river murmurs by;
    How soft the light, how full of balm
    The breeze that soothes the dark'ning sky!

    In every clime, in every state,
    We may be happy if we will;
    Man wrestles against iron fate,
    And then complains of pain and ill.

The secret of happiness lies in acceptance, says the poet Matthew Arnold. My struggle against the unchangeable tires and hurts me.

    Humble love
    And not proud reason, keeps the door of heaven.   AUGUST 19

EDWARD YOUNG

When we discover something of our real feelings it often seems   AUGUST 20
more like darkness than light, for our feelings will often not be the good and benevolent ones we thought they were. Yet paradoxically it is in that very darkness that God meets us and the darkness is the beginning of His light. For to see things as they are is to see them as God sees them.

HARRY WILLIAMS

AUGUST 21

From the desire of being praised, deliver me.
From the desire of being honoured, deliver me.
From the desire of being preferred, deliver me.
From the desire of being consulted, deliver me.
From the desire of being approved, deliver me.

This modern litany, author unknown, speaks to me because of my need to be approved and reassured by others. Arising out of low self-worth, this can distort all areas of my life, not just work.

AUGUST 22

Those who rush across the seas change the skies, not their own minds.

HORACE

AUGUST 23

Alone with none but Thee, my God
I journey on my way;
What need I fear, when Thou art near,
O King of night and day!
More safe am I within Thy hand
Than if a host did round me stand.

A prayer of St Columba, the Irish saint. Just before his death, the monastery's cart-horse put its head in the saint's lap and wept.

AUGUST 24

It is therefore our business carefully to cultivate in our minds, to rear to the most perfect vigour and maturity, every sort of generous and honest feeling that belongs to our nature.

EDMUND BURKE

Suppose flowers themselves were new!
Suppose they had just come into the world, a
sweet reward for some new goodness: and that
we had not yet seen them quite developed; that
they were in the act of growing; had just
issued with their green stalks out of the ground
and engaged the attention of the curious.
Imagine what we should feel when we saw the
first lateral stem bearing off from the main one,
or putting forth a leaf. Till at length in all its
fairy beauty, and odorous voluptuousness, and
mysterious elaboration of tender and living
sculpture shone forth 'the bright consummate
flower'! Yet this phenomenon, to a mind of
any thought and lovingness, is what may be
said to take place every day.

AUGUST 25

LEIGH HUNT

Seek out the good in every man,
And speak of all the best ye can;
Then will all men speak well of thee,
And say how kind of heart ye be.

AUGUST 26

GEOFFREY CHAUCER

AUGUST 27

There is a language wrote on earth and sky
By God's own pen in silent majesty;
There is a voice that's heard and felt and seen
In spring's young shades and summer's endless green;
Though no romantic scenes my feet have trod,
The voice of nature as the voice of God
Appeals to me in every tree and flower
Breathing his glory, magnitude and power.
In nature's open book I read, and see
Beauty's rich lesson in this seeming-pea;
And that small lark between me and the sky
Breathes sweetest strains of morning's melody;
Yet by the heedless crowd 'tis only heard
As the small warbling of a common bird.

JOHN CLARE

AUGUST 28   The highest form of wisdom is kindness.

BERAKOTH

AUGUST

God is love; and he that abideth in love abideth in God, and God abideth in him.

St John's first Epistle has this lovely sentence. When I am being truly loving to others and to myself, I must be close to God. And even when I am not loving, God's love for me does not diminish.

And truly, I reiterate, nothing's small!
No lily-muffled hum of a summer bee,
But finds some coupling with the spinning stars;
No pebble at your foot, but proves a sphere;
No chaffinch, but implies the cherubim.

ELIZABETH BARRETT BROWNING

There were times when I could not afford to sacrifice the bloom of the present moment to any work, whether of head or hands. Sometimes, in a summer morning, having taken my accustomed bath, I sat in my sunny doorway from sunrise till noon, rapt in a reverie, amidst the pines and hickories and sumachs, in undisturbed solitude and stillness, while the birds sang around. I grew in those seasons like corn in the night, and they were far better than any work of the hands would have been. They were not time subtracted from my life, but so much over and above my usual allowance.

The writings of Henry David Thoreau, the American philosopher, remind me that work and being busy is not as important as it often seems. Idleness, to recreate myself, is part of a properly balanced life.

SEPTEMBER

Do you not see how your Lord lengthens the shadows? Had it been His will He could have made them constant. But He makes the sun their guide; little by little he shortens them.

It is He who had made the night a mantle for you and sleep a rest. He makes each day a resurrection.

It is He who drives the winds as harbingers of His mercy and sends down pure water from the sky, so that He may give life to dead lands and quench the thirst of man and beast.

THE KORAN

In 1827 William Hone published The Table Book, *which contained a mixture of curious facts, some unusual poetry and his own reflections and advice to the reader. In it he listed 'Sentences worthy to be got by heart'. Here are some of them.*

As you cannot overtake time, the best way is to be always a few minutes before him.

Whatever your situation in life may be, lay down your plan of conduct for the day. The half hours will glide smoothly on, without crossing or jostling each other.

When you have set about a good work, do not rest till you have completed it.

In the morning think on what you are to do in the day, and at night, think on what you have done.

Do as you would be done by.

SEPTEMBER 3

The Hebrew prayer book has this prayer to be used on tasting fruit for the first time in the season. A prayer for apple and pear month.

Blessed art thou, O Lord our Good, King of the universe, who hast kept us in life, and hast preserved us, and hast enabled us to reach this season.

SEPTEMBER 4

Want is a bitter and a hateful good,
Because its virtues are not understood;
Yet many things, impossible to thought,
Have been by need to full perfection brought.
The daring of the soul proceeds from thence,
Sharpness of wit, and active diligence;
Prudence at once, and fortitude it gives;
And, if in patience taken, mends our lives.

These lines by John Dryden look at first sight rather grim. Yet in my life disappointments have turned out to be blessings in disguise. Often what I want is not at all the same as what I need.

SEPTEMBER

Mere enthusiasm is the all in all.

WILLIAM BLAKE

When all is done, learn this, my son,
Not friend, nor skill, nor wit at will,
Nor ship nor clod, but only God,
    Doth all in all:
Man taketh pain, God giveth gain,
Man doth his best, God doth the rest,
Man well intends, God foizon sends,
    Else want he shall.

In this sixteenth-century poem by Thomas Tusser to his son, the word 'foizon' means harvest. Tusser's poems, particularly the poems of advice for farmers, became well known. But poor Tusser, himself, was an unsuccessful farmer. Like most of us, he found it easier to give good advice to others than to follow it himself.

A thought transfixed me: for the first time in my life I saw the truth as it is set into song by so many poets, proclaimed as the final wisdom by so many thinkers. The truth – that love is the ultimate and the highest goal to which man can aspire. Then I grasped the meaning of the greatest secret that human poetry and human thought and belief have to impart: the salvation of man is through love and in love.

This extract comes from Man's Search for Meaning, *by Viktor Frankl, a moving book on how he lived through the concentration camp and the ways he made sense of that experience of hell.*

SEPTEMBER 8   Avoid all that you prove by experience or intuition to be wrong and you are safe; especially avoid the servile imitation of any other, be true to yourself, find out your own individuality and live and act in the circle around it.

Wise words from the philosopher John Stuart Mill. Self-distrust and fear of others' opinions is what stops me from being true to myself.

SEPTEMBER 9

There's music in the sighing of a reed;
There's music in the gushing of a rill;
There's music in all things, if men had ears;
Their earth is but an echo of the spheres.

LORD BYRON

SEPTEMBER 10   God made sun and moon to distinguish seasons, and day and night; and we cannot have the fruits of the earth but in their seasons. But God hath made no decree to distinguish the seasons of His mercies. In Paradise the fruits were ripe the first minute, and in Heaven it is always autumn, His mercies are ever in their maturity.

JOHN DONNE

SEPTEMBER 11

I am the image of God:
Therefore if God would see
Himself, He must look down
And see Himself in me.

ANGELUS SILESIUS

SEPTEMBER

Pleasures lie scattered all about our ways,
Harvest for thought and joy to look and glean.
Much of the beautiful to win our praise
Lie where we never heeded aught had been;
By this wood stile, half buried in the shade
Of rude disorder – bramble, woodbine, all
So thickly wove that nutters scarcely made
An entrance through – and now the acorns fall,
The gatherers seeking entrance pause awhile
Ere they mount up the bank to climb the stile,
Half wishing that a better road was nigh.
Yet here mid leaf-strewn mornings autumn mild,
While pleasing sounds and pleasing sights are bye
Things beautiful delight my heart to smile.

*For me this sonnet by John Clare, like so many
of his poems, is about the glory and the holiness
of very common ordinary things.*

Now is magical.

AUTHOR UNKNOWN

SEPTEMBER

<u>SEPTEMBER 14</u>

*Here is Christopher Smart's poem about late autumn
flowers.*

Ye beauties! O how great the sum
Of sweetness that ye bring;
On what a charity ye come
To bless the latter spring!
How kind a visit that ye pay,
Like strangers on a rainy day ...
Lo, through her works gay nature grieves
How brief she is and frail,
As ever o'er the falling leaves
Autumnal winds prevail.
Yet still the philosophic mind
Consolatory food can find,
And hope her anchorage maintain;
We never are deserted quite
'Tis by succession of delight
That love supports his reign.

<u>SEPTEMBER 15</u>   Draw nigh to God and he will draw nigh to you.

ST JAMES

SEPTEMBER

Wise men patience never want,
Good men pity cannot hide;
Feeble spirits only vaunt
Of revenge, the poorest pride.
He alone forgive that can,
Bears the true soul of a man.

SEPTEMBER 16

THOMAS CAMPION

Engineers make the water flow wherever they will; fletchers shape the arrow; carpenters carve the wood; wise people fashion themselves.

SEPTEMBER 17

This quotation comes from the Dhamapada, a Buddhist anthology of the fifth century BC. But to shape myself successfully, I must work with my own natural bent. Self-acceptance is necessary too.

Be not afraid to pray – to pray is right.
Pray, if thou canst, with hope; but ever pray,
Though hope be weak, or sick with long delay:
Pray in the darkness, if there be no light.

SEPTEMBER 18

HARTLEY COLERIDGE

One of my faults is that I am frightened of mistakes, of getting things wrong. Yet a truly good life requires a reckless willingness to make foolish errors. It therefore comforts me that the great scientist Sir Humphry Davy said this.

SEPTEMBER 19

The most important of my discoveries have been suggested to me by failures.

SEPTEMBER 20

If you think you are beaten, you are;
If you think you dare not, you don't;
If you want to win but think you can't
It's almost a cinch that you won't.

This verse, written by an unknown author, isn't true in all circum-stances but has some truth in it. As we think, so we act.

SEPTEMBER 21

Try to be happy in this very present moment; and put not off being so to a time to come: as though that time should be of another make from this, which is already come, and is ours.

THOMAS FULLER

SEPTEMBER 22

Through every minute of this day,
      Be with me, Lord!
Through every day of all this week,
      Be with me, Lord!

JOHN OXENHAM

SEPTEMBER 23

At his downfall the writer Oscar Wilde was deserted by his friends and sent to gaol. From Reading prison, he wrote this.

The important thing, the thing that lies before me, the thing I have to do, if the brief remainder of my days is not to be maimed, marred, and incomplete, is to absorb into my nature all that has been done to me, to make it part of me, to accept it without complaint, fear, or reluctance.

Animals can truly let go and let be and even celebrate without guilt feelings at 'wasted time' or at letting their masks down. Indeed, they instruct us in realizing that intensity of living is more important than duration and in this sense they cure us of the platonic prejudice humans have that declares that eternity and length of duration must be the test of the goodness of things.

Matthew Fox, author of A Spirituality Named Compassion, *is that rare being — a theologian who does justice to the other animals.*

SEPTEMBER 24

SEPTEMBER 25

Make no more pretences
Of new discoveries, whilst yet thine own,
And nearest, little world is still unknown.
Study thyself, and read what thou hast writ
In thine own book, thy conscience. Is it fit
To labour after knowledge so,
And thine own nearest, dearest, self not know?

CHRISTOPHER HARVEY

SEPTEMBER 26

Summer ends now; now, barbarous in beauty, the stooks
    arise
Around; up above, what wind⁄walks! what lovely
    behaviour
Of silk⁄sack clouds! has wilder, wilful⁄wavier
Meal⁄drift moulded ever and melted across skies?

I walk, I lift up, I lift up heart, eyes,
Down all that glory in the heavens to glean our Saviour;
And, éyes, héart, what looks, what lips yet gave you a
Rapturous love's greeting of realer, of rounder replies?

*The poet and priest, Gerard Manly Hopkins, writes poetry which goes
straight to the heart. Puzzling over meaning only hides it.*

SEPTEMBER 27

Grief can take care of itself, but to get the full value of a joy
you must have someone to divide it with.

MARK TWAIN

SEPTEMBER

Friendship is the gift of the gods, and the most precious boon to man.

BENJAMIN DISRAELI

> I lie where I have always lain,
> God smiles as he has always smiled:
> Ere suns and moons could wax and wane,
> Ere stars were thunder-girt or piled
> The heavens, God thought on me his child;
> Ordained a life for me, arrayed
> Its circumstances every one
> To the minutest: ay, God said
> This head this hand should rest upon
> Thus, ere he fashioned star or sun.
> And having thus created me,
> Thus rooted me, he bade me grow.

ROBERT BROWNING

Michael Faraday, the great chemist, gave a series of lectures, later published as a book with the title, The Chemical History of a Candle. *These are his closing words to the people listening.*

All I can say to you at the end of these lectures is to express a wish that you may, in your generation, be fit to compare to a candle; that you may, like it, shine as lights to those about you; that, in all your actions, you may justify the beauty of the taper by making your deeds honourable and effectual in the discharge of your duty to your fellow men.

OCTOBER

Over the great city,
Where the wind rustles through the parks and gardens,
In the air, the high clouds brooding,
In the lines of street perspective, the lamps, the traffic,
The pavements and the innumerable feet upon them,
I Am: make no mistake – do not be deluded.

Think not because I do not appear at the first glance –
    because the centuries have gone by and there is no
    assured tidings of me – that therefore I am not there.
Think not because all goes its own way that therefore I
    do not go my own way through all.
The fixed bent of hurrying faces in the street – each
    turned towards its own light, seeing no other – yet I
    am the Light towards which they all look.
The toil of so many hands to such multifarious ends,
    yet my hand knows the touch and twining of them
    all.

*This poem by Edward Carpenter moves me and somehow quietens my
anxieties. What I like is the idea that the divine is there for all of us,
in all of us, even in the bustle and grime of a great city.*

Health is the greatest of gifts, contentedness the best riches; trust
is the best of relationships.

THE BUDDHIST DHAMAPADA

OCTOBER 3

Endurance is the crowning quality,
And patience all the passion of great hearts.

JAMES RUSSELL LOWELL

OCTOBER 4

There are many tales about animals and Francis of Assisi, whose feast day is today. St Bonaventure, one of his biographers, tells of the saint's love for all living beings and their response to him.

He called all creatures, no matter how lowly, by the name of brother and sister, because, as far as he knew, they had sprung from the same original principle as himself ... Once when he was on his way in the neighbourhood of Sienna, he came upon a large flock of sheep in a field. When he had saluted them lovingly, as was his wont, they all left the pasture and came running to him, lifted their heads and fixed their eyes on him. So pleased did they seem with him that the shepherds and the friars were amazed, seeing not only ewes and lambs but even the rams so wonderfully gladdened.

Love God with all your soul and strength,
With all your heart and mind;
And love your neighbour as yourself;
Be faithful, just and kind.

This is a verse from Isaac Watts' Divine and Moral Songs for Children. *His improving verse is unfashionable, but I enjoy it.*

Whatever is best lies out of the reach of human power; can neither be given nor taken away. Such is this great and beautiful work of nature, the world. Such is the mind of man, which contemplates and admires the world, whereof it makes the noblest part. These are inseparably ours, and as long as we remain in one, we shall enjoy the other. Let us march, therefore, intrepidly wherever we are led by the course of human accidents.

LORD BOLINGBROKE

A day, a night, an hour of sweet content
Is worth a world consumed in fretful care.

Two lines from a poem by Thomas Campion. Sometimes I can make a deliberate effort to get back my peace of mind and let my fretting care go – take a holiday, however short, from worry.

Every visible and invisible creature is a theopany or appearance of God.

The medieval theologian, John Scotus Erigena, saw the glory of this world. With a sense of wonder it is impossible to be bored.

OCTOBER 9

Thou, who didst put to flight
Primeval silence, when the morning stars
Exulting shouted o'er the rising ball;
O Thou, whose word from solid darkness struck
That spark, the sun; strike wisdom from my soul!

EDWARD YOUNG

OCTOBER 10

The past is death's, the future is thine own. Take it while it is still yours, and fix your mind, not on what you may have done long ago to hurt, but on what you can now do to help.

I do not know where I came upon this passage by the poet Percy Bysshe Shelley. It means a great deal to me. I cannot undo my mistakes but I can try to make amends for them in some way now.

OCTOBER 11

When seasons change, then lay before thine eyes
His wondrous method; mark the various scenes
In heav'n; hail, thunder, rainbows, snow and ice,
Calms, tempests, light and darkness by His means;
Thou canst not miss His praise; each tree, herb,
  flower
Are shadows of His wisdom and His power.

HENRY VAUGHAN

OCTOBER 12

To love God truly, you must first love man, and if anyone tells you that he loves God but does not love his fellow men, he is lying.

HASIDIC SAYING

OCTOBER

Do you want to be really happy? You can begin by being appreciative of who you are and what you've got. Do you want to be really miserable? You can begin by being discontented. As Lao-tse wrote: 'A tree as big around as you can reach starts with a small seed; a thousand-mile journey starts with one step.' Wisdom, Happiness and Courage are not waiting somewhere out beyond sight at the end of a straight line; they're part of a continuous cycle that begins right here.

More wisdom from Benjamin Hoff's odd book, The Tao of Pooh.

'Tis pleasant and we think it fine,
To spend our time on a design
To get some honour, and increase
Our wealth, till the hour of our decease;
Not using what we do possess,
In hopes to gain more happiness.
Thus for some nothing, or a toy,
We lose the time we might enjoy.

SIR WILLIAM KILLIGREW

OCTOBER 15 Suppose a river, or a drop of water, an apple or a sand, an ear of corn, or an herb. God knoweth infinite excellencies in it more than we; He seeth how it relateth to angels and men; how it representeth all His attributes; how it conduceth in its place, by the best of means to the best of ends: and for this cause it cannot be beloved too much. God the Author and God the End are to be beloved in it; angels and men are to be beloved in it; and it is highly to be esteemed for all their sakes.

Who can love anything that God made too much?

THOMAS TRAHERNE

OCTOBER 16 When some great sorrow like a mighty river
Flows through your life with peace-destroying power,
And the dearest things are swept from sight for ever,
Say to yourself each trying hour,
'This too will pass away.'

AUTHOR UNKNOWN

Farewell, complaint, the miser's only pleasure:
Away, vain cares, by which few men do find
Their sought-for treasure.

SIR PHILIP SIDNEY

OCTOBER 17

The joy which a man finds in his work and which transforms the tears and sweat of it into happiness and delight – that joy is God. The wonder and curiosity which welcomes what is new and regards it not as threatening but enriching life – that wonder and curiosity is God.

HARRY WILLIAMS

OCTOBER 18

I am so fond of the poetry of John Clare that I could fill each day with it. Here is the start of his poem, 'A Look At The Heavens'.

OCTOBER 19

Oh, who can witness with a careless eye
The countless lamps that light an evening sky,
And not be struck with wonder at the sight!
To think what mighty Power must there abound,
That burns each spangle with a steady light,
And guides each hanging world its rolling round.

Live your life while you have it. Life is a splendid gift. There is nothing small in it. For the greatest things grow by God's law out of the smallest.

FLORENCE NIGHTINGALE

OCTOBER 20

OCTOBER 21

Ere on my bed my limbs I lay,
It hath not been my use to pray
With moving lips or bended knees,
But silently, by slow degrees,
My spirit I to Love compose,
In humble trust mine eyelids close.

A lovely description by Samuel Taylor Coleridge of how he prayed.

OCTOBER 22

It seems to me we can never give up longing and wishing while we are thoroughly alive. There are certain things we feel to be beautiful and good, and we must hunger after them.

This passage comes in one of George Eliot's novels. I can aim at contentment, but not at the risk of settling for less than I should.

OCTOBER 23

We have within ourselves
Enough to fill the present day with joy,
And overspread the future years with hope.

WILLIAM WORDSWORTH

OCTOBER 24

You may regard your work as dull and unromantic, but actually it is made that way if the person who works at that job becomes dull. Try this experiment. For one day think no drab thoughts about your job. Look deeply into its possibilities. Think big and exciting thoughts about it. I believe that just one day of this will surprise you.

NORMAN VINCENT PEALE

O soul, canst thou not under-
stand
Thou art not left alone,
As a dog to howl and moan
His master's absence. Thou art
as a book
Left in a room that He forsook,
But returns to by and by,
A book of His dear choice —
That quiet waiteth for His
hand,
That quiet waiteth for His eye,
That quiet waiteth for His
voice.

MICHAEL FIELD

OCTOBER 25

Ralph Waldo Emerson is so often quoted that cynics treat him as a joke. Yet his essays are full of exciting and liberating ideas.

OCTOBER 26

The beauty that shimmers in the yellow afternoons of October, who ever could clutch it? Go forth to find it and it is gone; 'tis only a mirage as you look from the windows of diligence. The presence of a higher, namely, of the spiritual element is essential to its perfection.

OCTOBER 27

Seek no more abroad, say I,
House and home, but turn thine eye
Inward, and observe thy breast;
There alone dwells solid rest.
Say not that this house is small,
Girt up in a narrow wall;
In a cleanly sober mind
Heaven itself full room doth find.

JOSEPH BEAUMONT

OCTOBER 28 *Benjamin Franklin made a list of virtues and resolutions and then tried to make each virtue a habit. Here are some of them.*

Order. Let all your things have their places; let each part of your business have its time.

Sincerity. Use not hurtful deceit; think innocently and justly, and, if you speak, speak accordingly.

Tranquillity. Be not disturbed at trifles, or at accidents common or unavoidable.

Unthinking heads, who have not learned to be alone are in a prison to themselves. Be able to be alone. Lose not the advantage of solitude and the society of thyself. He who is thus prepared, the day is not uneasy nor the night black unto him.

I do not find this advice from Sir Thomas Browne easy to follow. When I cannot bear my own company, usually I have slipped into self-hatred. I have forgotten to look after my own inner health.

Ten thousand thousand precious gifts
My daily thanks employ,
Nor is the least a cheerful heart,
That tastes those gifts with joy.

JOSEPH ADDISON

Today is Hallowe'en, a day when I remember those I loved who have died. I try to trust that somehow, despite death, all is well. This passage, which I love, was written by William Penn.

Death cannot kill what never dies. Nor can spirits ever be divided that love and live in the same divine principle; the root and record of their friendship. If absence be not death, neither is it theirs. Death is but crossing the world, as friends do the seas; they lie in one another still. For they must needs be present that love and live in that which is omnipresent. This is the comfort of friends, that though they may be said to die, yet their friendship and society are, in the best sense, ever present because immortal.

WILLIAM PENN

NOVEMBER

The quiet childhood of humanity, spent in the far-off forest glades, and by the murmuring rivers, is done for ever; and human life is deepening down to manhood amidst tumult, doubt and hope. Its age of restful peace is past. It has its work to finish, and must hasten on. What that work may be – what this world's share is in the great Design – we know not, though our unconscious hands are helping to accomplish it. Like the tiny coral insect working deep under the dark waters, we strive and struggle each for our own little ends, nor dream of the vast Fabric we are building up for God. Let us have done with vain regrets and longings for the days that never will be ours again. Our work lies in front, not behind us; and 'Forward!' is our motto.

JEROME K. JEROME

There is an Eye that never sleeps,
Beneath the wind of night.
There is an Ear that never shuts,
When sinks the beams of light.
There is an Arm that never tires,
When human strength gives way.
There is a Love that never fails,
When earthly loves decay.

GEORGE MATHESON

NOVEMBER 3   A certain man was going down from Jerusalem to Jericho; and he fell among thieves, which stripped him of his raiment and wounded him, and departed, leaving him half dead.

And by chance there came down a certain priest that way: and when he saw him, he passed by on the other side.

And likewise a Levite, when he was at that place, came and looked on him, and passed by on the other side.

But a certain Samaritan, as he journeyed, came where he was: and when he saw him, he had compassion on him.

And went to him, and bound up his wounds, pouring in oil and wine; and set him on his own beast, and brought him to an inn, and took care of him ...

Which now of these three, thinkest thou, was neighbour unto him that fell among the thieves?

JESUS OF NAZARETH

NOVEMBER

A cheerful but an upright heart
Is music wheresoe're thou art.

OWEN FELTHAM

May the lines of love meet in your heart.

IRISH BLESSING

Hardy clowns! grudge not the wheat
Which hunger forces birds to eat:
Your blinded eyes, worst foes to you,
Can't see the good which sparrows do.
Did not poor birds with watching rounds
Pick up the insects from your grounds,
Did they not tend your rising grain,
You then might sow to reap in vain.
Thus Providence, right understood,
Whose end and aim is doing good,
Sends nothing here without its use;
Though ignorance loads it with abuse –
O God, let me what's good pursue,
Let me the same to others do
As I'd have others do to me
And learn at least humanity.

JOHN CLARE

Be patient, love yourself, and miracles will happen.

CHRISTINA CALDWELL

NOVEMBER 8

Knowledge and wisdom, far from being one,
Have ofttimes no connection. Knowledge dwells
In heads replete with thoughts of other men:
Wisdom in minds attentive to their own.
Knowledge, a rude unprofitable mass,
The mere materials with which wisdom builds,
Till smoothed and squared and fitted to its place,
Does but encumber whom it seems t'enrich.

I find it easy to confuse knowledge and wisdom so these lines by William Cowper remind me that they are not the same. It is so much easier for me to be clever and knowing, than to be wise.

NOVEMBER 9

When friendships are real, they are not glass threads of frost-work, but the solidest thing we know.

RALPH WALDO EMERSON

NOVEMBER 10

See in every hedgerow
Marks of angels' feet,
Epics in each pebble
Underneath our feet.

CHARLES KINGSLEY

NOVEMBER 11

Almighty God, from whom all thoughts of truth and peace proceed: kindle, we pray thee, in the hearts of all men the true love of peace.

For the day when the First World War ended, a prayer by Francis Paget. If I truly value peace I must have an attitude of 'live and let live'.

NOVEMBER

NOVEMBER 12

Hartley Coleridge was a minor poet, the son of a greater one. I like the message of his poems. This one is addressed to a baby.

> The Christian virtues, one, two three,
> Faith and hope and charity,
> May all find exercise in thee.
>
> In faith, sweet infant that thou art,
> Of God's sublime decrees a part,
> Thy mother holds thee to her heart.
>
> Hope is the joy of faith. It were
> Sad to behold a babe so fair
> Without the hope that makes a joy of care.
>
> Well 'twill be if we can learn,
> If loving thee, babe, we discern
> The love of God, and let it clearly burn.

NOVEMBER 13

Do your own work and know yourself.

PLATO

NOVEMBER 14

From the seed of contentment a harvest of peace is reaped.
Break the clods with the staff of love,
That the damp of envy may not remain beneath:
From the seed of contentment a harvest of peace is reaped.

NAND RAM

NOVEMBER 15

We are in such haste to be doing, to be writing, to be gathering gear, to make our voice audible a moment in the derisive silence of eternity, that we forget that one thing, of which these are but the parts – namely to live. We fall in love, we drink hard, we run to and fro upon the earth like frightened sheep. And now you are to ask yourself if, when all is done, you would not have been better to sit by the fire and home and be happy thinking.

This passage by Robert Louis Stevenson is important for me. I am often so busy rushing through my life that I forget to pause, to take stock, to enjoy it. Always being busy is not living fully.

NOVEMBER

Let honesty be as the breath of thy soul.

BENJAMIN FRANKLIN

This dark and wet month of year can be enjoyed. In the rough winds and bare trees Robert Burns could feel nature's beauty.

> Ev'n winter bleak has charms to me,
> When winds rave thro' the naked tree;
> Or frosts on hills of Ochiltree
> > Are hoary gray;
> Or blinding drifts wild-furious flee,
> > Dark'ning the day!

If one advances confidently in the direction of his dreams, and endeavours to live the life which he has imagined, he will meet with a success unexpected in common hours.

HENRY DAVID THOREAU

Here is some anonymous inspiration which a friend passed on to me.

> God make me a little bit kinder,
> A little more tender and true,
> Not needing constant reminder
> Of the things that I know I should do.
> God make me more easy to live with
> Less ready to get hurt and vexed,
> More patient and helpful in dealing
> With the worried, the sad, the perplexed.

NOVEMBER 20

Stop, where does thou run?
God's heaven is in thee.
If thou seekest it elsewhere
Never shalt thou see.

ANGELUS SILESIUS

NOVEMBER 21

There is nothing in this world worth doing a mean action for; much less an injust one.

This sentence comes from the 1799 memoirs of Major Thomas Oldfield. It was the simple faith of a very gallant Royal Marine.

NOVEMBER 22

Today is the feast day of St Cecilia, patron saint of music; let us then celebrate in the words of Thomas Campion its various powers for good. This song was sung during the King's supper.

Tune thy cheerful voice to mine,
Music helps digesting.
Music is as good as wine,
And as fit for feasting.
Joy at thy board, health in thy dish,
Mirth in thy cup, and in thy bed
Soft sleep and pleasing rest we wish.

NOVEMBER 23

Crush not yonder ant as it draggeth along its grain; for it too liveth, and its life is sweet to it. A shadow there must be, and a stone upon that heart, that could wish to sorrow the heart even of an ant!

SHEIKH MUSLIH ADDIN SADI

Blessed of the Lord be his land, for the precious things of heaven, for the dew, and for the deep that coucheth beneath,

And for the precious fruits brought forth by the sun, and for the precious things brought forth by the moon,

And for the chief things of the ancient mountains, and for the precious things of the lasting hills,

And for the precious things of the earth and fulness thereof.

DEUTERONOMY

Too much thinking doth consume the spirits, and oft it falls out, that while one thinks too much of doing, he leaves to do the effect of his thinking.

This shrewd judgement was made by Sir Philip Sidney. I am often obsessed about difficulties, thus using up energy which might be better spent on action. And there are some problems that require my heart's deep acceptance, rather than my brain's clever thinking.

NOVEMBER 26

Only life's common plod: still to repair
The body and the thing which perisheth:
The soil, the smutch, the toil and ache and wear,
The grinding enginry of blood and breath,
Pain's random darts, the heartless spade of death;
All is but grief and heavily we call
On the last terror for the end of all.

Then comes the happy moment: not a stir
In any tree, no portent in the sky:
The morning doth neither hasten nor defer,
The morrow hath no name to call it by,
But life and joy are one — we know not why —
As though our very blood long breathless lain
Had tasted of the breath of God again.

ROBERT BRIDGES

NOVEMBER 27   The worship of God is honouring his gifts in other men ...
Those who envy or calumniate great men hate God.

WILLIAM BLAKE

Thou wilt never have any quiet if thou vexest thyself, because thou canst not bring mankind to that exact notion of things and rule of life which thou hast formed in thy own mind.

THOMAS FULLER

No matter who I am
Or where I've been,
No matter what I've done
Or what I've seen;

No matter what I have
Or where I go,
No matter what I do
Or how I grow;

God will direct me,
God will correct me,
God will protect me,
God will accept me.

I found these three simple verses by John Stuart comforting and reassuring when I heard them read in an old Somerset church.

Affability, mildness, tenderness, and a word which I would fain bring back to its original signification of virtue, I mean good nature, are of daily use; they are the bread of mankind and the staff of life.

JOHN DRYDEN

DECEMBER

Though now no more the musing ear
Delights to listen to the breeze,
That lingers o'er the green wood shade,
I love thee, winter, well.

Not undelightful now to roam
The wild heath sparkling on the sight;
Not undelightful now to pace
The forest's ample rounds

And see the spangled branches shine,
And mark the moss of many a hue
That varies the old tree's brown bark,
And o'er the grey stone spreads.

The green moss shines with icy glare;
The long grass bends its spear-like form;
And lovely is the silvery scene
When fain the sunbeams smile.

Robert Southey wrote these verses on 1 December in 1793.

Life has meaning only in the struggle. Triumph and defeat are in the hands of the gods. So let us celebrate the struggle.

This is part of a Swahili song, motto for the film, 'Lorenzo's Oil'.

<u>DECEMBER 3</u> *Henry Vaughan wrote this lovely poem. Its title is 'The Bird'.*

Hither thou com'st: the busy wind all night
Blew through thy lodging, where thy own warm wing
Thy pillow was. Many a sullen storm –
For which coarse man seems much the fitter born –
  Rained on thy bed
  And harmless head:

And now as fresh and cheerful as the light
Thy little heart in early hymns doth sing
Unto that Providence, Whose unseen arm
Curbed them, and clothed thee well and warm.
  All things that be, praise Him: and had
  Their lesson taught them when first made.

So hills and valleys into singing break;
And though poor stones have neither speech nor tongue,
While active winds and streams both run and speak,
Yet stones are deep in admiration.
Thus praise and prayer here beneath the sun
Make lesser mornings, when the great are done.

DECEMBER

The spacious firmament on high,
With all the blue ethereal sky,
And spangled heav'ns, a shining frame,
Their great Original proclaim...
Soon as the evening shades prevail,
The moon takes up the wondrous tale,
And nightly to the list'ning earth
Repeats the story of her birth.

Joseph Addison's hymn is best enjoyed outside on a frosty night.

Do good with what thou hast, or it will do thee no good. If thou wouldst be happy, bring thy mind to thy condition, and have an indifferency for more than what is sufficient. Be rather bountiful than expensive.

WILLIAM PENN

The first sure symptom of a mind in health,
Is rest of heart, and pleasure felt at home.

EDWARD YOUNG

God is in every experience of the world. For those who fear the impossibility of such things, there is always one way through their tunnel. It is to believe that it is a tunnel. That there is a light at the end. That it is worth waiting, that it is wise to be open to all new ideas, all new impressions.

This comes from an anthology, Dust Glorified *by Anne Shells.*

DECEMBER 8

Not from his fellows only man may learn
Rights to compare and duties to discern!
All creatures and all objects, in degree,
Are friends and patrons of humanity.
There are to whom the garden, grove, and field
Perpetual lessons of forbearance yield;
Who would not lightly violate the grace
The lowliest flower possesses in its place.

WILLIAM WORDSWORTH

DECEMBER 9 Each day is a little life.

ARTHUR SCHOPENHAUER

DECEMBER 10 *Alfred, Lord Tennyson wrote these hopeful lines in an old inn at London's Temple Bar when his fortunes were at their lowest.*

Let there be thistles, there are grapes;
If old things, there are new;
Ten thousand broken lights and shapes,
Yet glimpses of the true ...
High over roaring Temple Bar,
And set in heaven's third story,
I look at all things as they are,
But through a kind of glory.

DECEMBER 11 If a man would move the world, he must first move himself.

SOCRATES

St Francis of Assisi loved all creation, and believed that animals, both wild and tame, should not be left out of winter feasting.

All civic authorities and the lords of fortresses and villages should be asked every year, on the day of the nativity of Our Lord, to compel the people to scatter corn and other grains on the roads outside the towns and castles, so that our sisters the larks and the other birds should have enough to eat on that most solemn festival; and that, out of reverence for the Son of God, who on that night was laid in the manger by the Blessed Virgin Mary between an ox and an ass, whoever has an ox and an ass, should provide them with a good feed that night.

DECEMBER 13   *The writer Leigh Hunt wrote a short essay on 'Rules in Making Presents'. Christmas shopping can be a chance to express love.*

If you are rich, it is a good rule in general to make a rich present. On the other hand, a poor man, if he is generous, and understood to be so, may make the very poorest of presents and give it an exquisite value; for his heart and his understanding will accompany it. With no sort of presents must there be pretence. People must not say (and say falsely) that they could get no other, or that they could afford no better; nor must they affect to think better of the present than it is worth; nor, above all, keep asking about it after it is given – how you like it, whether you find it useful, etc. To receive a present handsomely and in a right spirit, even when you have none to give in return, is to give one in return.

DECEMBER 14   'Tis mine the passing hour to tell.
                                       'Tis thine to use it ill or well.

                            INSCRIPTION ON AN OLD CLOCK

DECEMBER

The way to God is by thy self. The height of all philosophy, both natural and moral, is to know thy self, and the end of this knowledge is to know God.

This passage was written by Francis Quarles, a seventeenth-century poet. When I gained some real understanding of myself, I discovered, to my surprise, that it renewed my spiritual life.

All truths wait in all things,
They neither hasten their own delivery nor resist it,
They do not need the obstetric forceps of the surgeon,
The insignificant is as big to me as any,
(What is less or more than a touch?)

Logic and sermons never convince,
The damp of the night drives deeper into my soul.

Walt Whitman's lines tell me to stop trying to force solutions, to stop having to make sense of everything — just to be and accept.

At Christmas we should remember that children have a special spirituality to teach us. The poet Francis Thompson describes it.

Know you what it is to be a child? It is to be something very different from the man of today. It is to believe in love, to believe in loveliness, to believe in belief: it is to be so little that the elves can reach to whisper in your ear; it is to turn pumpkins into coaches, and mice into horses, lowness into loftiness, and nothing into everything, for each child has its fairy godmother in its soul.

DECEMBER 18   In order that people may be happy in their work, these three things are needed: they must be fit for it; they must not do too much of it; and they must have a sense of success in it.

I like John Ruskin's thoughts on work, because I have difficulty in that area. I need to remember not to do too much, to take proper rest, and also to take proper recreation from work.

DECEMBER 19   God, the spirit of creativity and genius,
Made us curious, eager and determined.
With special talents to be discovered in
     ourselves and in each other,
And we are given clarity, gentleness and
     friendliness
To help us.

A friend of mine has these lines on a wallet card. They were written by Robert Lefever who runs a treatment centre for alcoholics and drug addicts. The lines encourage self-discovery.

DECEMBER 20   What you practise, you learn; what you learn, you become.

AUTHOR UNKNOWN

DECEMBER 21   May the faith that gives us hope,
May the love that shows the way,
May the peace that cheers the heart,
Be yours this day.

AUTHOR UNKNOWN

DECEMBER

Lord, I am like to mistletoe,
Which has no root, and cannot grow
Or prosper but by that same tree
It clings about; so I by Thee.
What need I then to fear at all,
So long as I about Thee crawl?

ROBERT HERRICK

DECEMBER 22

Can you take too much joy in your Father's works? He is him⁄ self in everything. Some things are little on the outside, and rough and common, but I remember the time when the dust of the streets was as precious as gold to my infant eyes, and now it is more precious to the eye of reason.

THOMAS TRAHERNE

DECEMBER 23

DECEMBER

DECEMBER 24

A frosty Christmas Eve
  when stars were shining
Fared I forth alone
  where westward falls the hill
And from many a village
  in the watered valley
Distant music reached me
  peals of bells aringing ...
But to me heard afar
  it was starry music
Angels' song, comforting
  as the comfort of Christ
When he spake tenderly
  to his sorrowful flock:
The old words came to me
  by the riches of time
Mellowed and transfigured
  as I stood on the hill
Heark'ning in the aspect
  of th'eternal silence.

ROBERT BRIDGES

DECEMBER 25

Poor world, said I, what wilt thou do
To entertain this starry stranger?
Is this the best thou canst bestow —
A cold and not-too-cleanly manger?
Contend, the powers of heaven and earth,
To fit a bed for this huge birth.

Welcome all wonders in one sight!
Eternity shut in a span!
Summer in winter! day in night!
Heaven in earth! and God in man!
Great little one, whose all-embracing birth
Lifts earth to heaven, stoops heaven to earth.

RICHARD CRAWSHAW

DECEMBER 26

I have a fondness for the poet George Wither, whose life in the seven-teenth century was full of misfortunes, often self-inflicted! He wrote this passage on the true purpose of Christmas feasting.

This day is worthily dedicated to be observed in remembrance of the blessed nativity of our redeemer, Jesus Christ; at which time it pleased the Almighty Father to send his only begotten Son into the world for our sakes. To express therefore our thankfulness, and the joy we ought to have in this love of God, there hath been anciently, and is yet continued, a neighbourly and plentiful hospitality in inviting, and (without invitation) receiving unto our well-furnished tables, our tenants, neigh-bours, friends and strangers; to the increase of amity and free-hearted kindness among us.

DECEMBER 27   It is the God in all that is our companion and friend, for our God himself says: 'You are my brother, my sister, and my mother', and St John: 'Whoso dwelleth in love dwelleth in God and God in him.' God is in the lowest effects as well as the highest causes; for he is become a worm that he may nourish the weak.

WILLIAM BLAKE

DECEMBER 28

Come to me, beloved,
Babe of Bethlehem;
Lay aside Thy sceptre
And Thy diadem.

Bid all fear and doubting
From my soul depart,
As I feel the beating
Of Thy human heart.

Look upon me sweetly
With Thy human eyes,
With Thy human finger
Point me to the skies.

DIGBY MACKWORTH DOLBEN

DECEMBER 29   Some of the happiest creatures I know are animals and they do not hesitate to demonstrate their joy at living.

As Matthew Fox points out, we can learn the simplest joy of all from animals. This joy is something I need to cultivate every day.

DECEMBER

The world is not to be learned and thrown aside, but reverted to and relearned.

I find a great deal of hope in this sentence by Robert Browning. If I cannot learn from an experience now, perhaps I can learn later, or relearn still later. So failure is of no great account.

O God of Love, we pray Thee to give us love;
Love in our thinking, love in our speaking,
Love in our doing,
And love in the hidden places of our souls;
Love of our neighbours near and far;
Love of our friends, old and new;
Love of those with whom we
    find it hard to bear,
And love of those who find it hard
    to bear with us;
Love of those with whom we work,
And love of those with whom we take
    our ease;
Love in joy, love in sorrow,
Love in life and love in death;
That so at length we may be worthy to dwell
    with Thee,
Who art eternal Love.

WILLIAM TEMPLE

ACKNOWLEDGEMENTS

I have tried to obtain permission from copyright holders to reproduce the quotations in this book, but there are some I could not trace. The publishers will be happy to rectify any omissions in future editions. I should like to thank the following for permission to reprint:

The Andrew Young Estate for an extract from *A Retrospect of Flowers* by Andrew Young, Jonathan Cape Ltd.

Bear and Company, for extracts reprinted from *Whee! We, Wee All the Way Home*, by Matthew Fox, Copyright © 1981, Bear & Co Inc., P.O. Box 2860, Santa Fé, NM 87504.

Hazel Charlton for an extract from 'I listen' from *Come and Praise*, published by BBC Enterprises Ltd.

Constable & Co Ltd and Mary Martin for an extract from *Beasts and Saints* by Helen Waddell, Constable and Co Ltd; the Revd Harry Williams and Constable & Co Ltd for extracts from *The True Wilderness* by Harry Williams, published by Constable & Co Ltd.

Darton Longman and Todd Ltd and the Anglican Book Centre, Toronto, Ontario, for an extract from *God of Surprises* by Gerald Hughes, Darton Longman and Todd, and with permission from St Pauls, P.B. 9814 58/23rd Rd, T.P. S. 111, Bandra, Bombay–400 050, India.

Bob Earll, c/o Recovery Enterprises, London, for 'Children are not put here for us to teach'.

Faber and Faber Ltd for an extract from *Diary of a Russian Priest* by Alexander Elchaninov.

Harper Collins Publishers, for extracts from *A Spirituality Named Compassion* by Matthew Fox. Copyright © 1979 by Matthew Fox. Reprinted by permission of Harper Collins, Publishers.

Harvard University Press for 'Spring is the Period' and 'Nature is what we see' by Emily Dickinson. Reprinted by permission of the publishers and the Trustees of Amherst College from *The Poems of Emily Dickinson*, Thomas H. Johnson, ed., Cambridge, Massachusetts; The Belknap Press of Harvard University Press, Copyright © 1951, 1955, 1979, l983 by the President and Fellows of Harvard College.

Hodder Headline plc and Beacon Press for an extract from *Man's Search for Meaning* by Viktor Frankl. Copyright © 1959, 1962, 1992 by Viktor E. Frankl. Reprinted by permission of Beacon Press.

Sophie Kullmann c/o Celia Haddon for 'Love is like a Blossom'.

Dr Robert Lefever of the PROMIS Recovery Centre, The Old Court House, Pinners Hill, Nonington, Kent CT 15 4LL for the PROMIS wallet cardprayer.

Macmillan London Ltd for an extract from *A Book of School Worship* by William Temple and 'The Bright Field' and 'Song' from *Later Poems* by R.S. Thomas.

Kevin Mayhew Ltd for 'Do not be afraid' by Gerard Markland, copyright © Kevin Mayhew Ltd. Used by permission, from Hymns *Old and New*, License No. 397031.

Mid Northumberland Arts Group and Carcanet Press for 'The Clump of Fern' and 'A Morning Walk' from *The Midsummer Cushion*, edited by Anne Tibble.

Penguin Books Ltd for 'Al-Furqan' (pp 255–256) from *The Koran* translated by N.J. Dawood (Penguin Classics), fifth revised edition 1990 copyright © N.J. Dawood, 1956, 1959, 1966, 1968, 1974, 1990.

Penguin Books USA for 'Self-Pity', 'Many Mansions' and 'Know Thyself', from *The Complete Poems of D.H. Lawrence* by D.H. Lawrence, edited by V. de Sola Pinto and F.W. Roberts. Copyright © 1964, 1971 by Angelo Ravagli and C.M. Weekley, Executors of the Estate of Frieda Lawrence Ravagli. Used by permission of Viking Penguin, a division of Penguin USA.

The Revd Dudley Ractliffe for 'Lord, you know'.

Random House, Inc. for an extract from *Tales of the Hasidim: The Early Masters*, by Martin Buber. Copyright © 1947,1948, and renewed 1975 by Schocken Books, Inc. Reprinted by permission of Schocken Books, published by Pantheon Books, a division of Random House, Inc.

R.I. B. Library and Penguin Books USA for an extract from *The Tao of Pooh* by Benjamin Hoff, published by Methuen Childrens Books. Copyright © 1982 Benjamin Hoff: text and illus. from *Winnie the Pooh* and *The House at Pooh Corner* CR 1926, 1928 by E.P. Dutton, copyright © 1953, 1956 by A.A. Milne. Used by permission of Dutton Signet, a division of Penguin USA.

George T. Sassoon for 'Who's this – alone with stone and sky?' by Siegfried Sassoon, by permission of George T. Sassoon.

Sheed and Ward Ltd for extracts from *St Francis of Assisi* edited by Otto Karrer, translated by N. Wydenbruck, published by Sheed and Ward Ltd.

Shoreline Books for an extract from *Dust Glorified* by Anne Shells, published in 1992 by Shoreline Books, 11 Colston Yard, Colston St, Bristol BS1 5BD.

Simon and Schuster for an extract from *Stay Alive All Your Life* by Norman Vincent Peale, published in the UK by Cedar Books, Heinemann, copyright © 1957, 1985. Reprinted by permission of the publisher, Prentice-Hall, Inc. a division of Simon and Schuster, Englewood Cliffs, N.J.

The Society of Authors as the literary representative of the Estate of John Masefield, for 'He who gives a child a treat.'

Trevor Stephens of the Lani Memorial Trust, P.O. Box 3767, Alice Spring, NT0871, Australia, for the story of Garuda and the sparrow.

The Revd John Stuart for lines from 'Free to Be'.

PICTURE CREDITS

Joyce Haddon: title page, 12 April, 13 June. Fine Art Photographs: January – *Driving Home the Flock*, Thomas Smythe; February – *Spring Flowers*, Henry James Johnstone; March – *Spring Decorations*, Agnes Gardner King; April – *An April Afternoon*, Edward Wilkins Waite; May – *The Bluebell Glade*, Ernest Walbourn; June – *The Path by the Water Lane*, Myles Birket Foster; July – *A Swing of Love*, William Strutt; August – *Cullercoats Cliffs*, Myles Birket Foster; September – *A Haymaker at Rest*, Charles Edward Wilson; October – *An Autumn Lane*, Edward Wilkins Waite; November – *Cutting Bracken*, Henry Herbert La Thangue; December – *Christmas Eve*, George Bernard O'Neill.